Ranger Rick's
ANSWER

National Wildlife Federation

Library of Congress CIP Data: page 95.

BOOK

FLY THIS WAY FOR FUN!

Inspired by RANGER RICK'S NATURE MAGAZINE

Has anyone ever seen the start of a new volcano?

Yes! Here is a true story about one of them.

Early in 1943, a farmer plowing his corn field near a village in southern Mexico became frightened. An earthquake was shaking the ground all around him very hard.

Smoke, gray ash, a hissing noise like that made by water splashing onto a hot skillet, and the rotten-egg smell of sulfur gases poured from a crack in the ground. The farmer was watching the birth of a volcano!

Lava-covered church. San Juan. Mexico. 1952

By evening the crack had opened several feet. Red-hot liquid rock called *lava* erupted from the crack. The lava flew high into the air and cooled in small pieces called *cinders*. They started piling up to form a black, smoking, cone-shaped hill.

And how it grew! By the end of the first week the volcano was nearly as tall as a 50-story skyscraper.

Nine years later, the volcano stopped erupting. It had grown to be a mountain over a quarter mile (420 m) high.

THE GOOSE THAT LIVES IN A VOLCANO

On the Hawaiian island Maui (MAU-ee), a species of goose lives in an inactive volcano named Haleakala (ha-lee-ah-KAH-lah). No one really knows how the geese got there. Scientists guess that thousands of years ago

a flock of Canada geese got lost while migrating. A bad storm may have blown them way off course and a few of them landed on Haleakala. The geese stayed there, maybe because they liked the food.

Over the years the geese changed. Today these birds, called *nene* (nay-nay) geese, no longer look like Canada geese. They climb up and down the rocky walls of the volcano, so their legs have become stronger and the webs on their feet have become smaller. Because Hawaii is warm all year, the birds no longer have to migrate over long distances and their wings have become smaller. In time, even the markings on their feathers changed.

Are there any volcanoes under the oceans?

Yes. On November 14, 1963, about 20 miles off the coast of Iceland, the night was shattered by huge explosions from under the ocean floor. Great tongues of fire shot up through the water. The air was filled with steam and flying ash.

Although the sea was over 425 feet deep, the explosions came up in great bursts through the green water. Chunks of the earth's crust, some as big as a car, were hurled thousands of feet into the air. The fireworks kept up all through that winter and into the spring of 1964. The eruption was the longest one known in the area in a thousand years.

The explosions stopped in April, 1964. Then lava poured out of the volcano. By winter, the lava had built up into a rocky island 400 feet above the waves and about a mile square. The Icelanders named the new island "Surtsey," after a legendary Icelandic fire giant.

6

Lava

What causes volcanoes?

The center of the earth is so hot that it melts rock. This liquid rock, called *magma,* rises toward the earth's surface. In most places the earth's crust holds it in. Sometimes the magma finds a weak place in the crust and bursts through as a volcano. At other times, an earthquake may weaken or break the crust and let the hot lava and gases escape in a volcanic eruption.

Core
Mantle
Crust

Were all the continents once joined together?

Probably. Many scientists believe that over 200 million years ago all the continents were part of one huge piece of land surrounded by water. That land slowly broke apart and the pieces drifted away from each other. They formed the continents of Eurasia (Europe and Asia), Africa, North America, South America, Antarctica, and Australia.

Look at a map of the world. Don't some of the continents look as if they were pieces of a jigsaw puzzle that would fit together? Notice South America and Africa. They look as though they would join perfectly—if only they could be moved across the ocean. Well, once they probably *were* joined.

Can the continents move?

Yes. At least two clues help us understand how continents can move. One is that the earth's outer layer, the crust, is broken up into about ten separate pieces called *plates.* These plates lie on top of the mantle, the layer of rocks between the earth's crust and its core. The continents are part of the plates. The other clue is this: although the mantle is very hard near the core, it is soft near the crust. The plates can actually slide across the top of the mantle. Some scientists believe that melted rock (magma) pushing up between the plates forces them (and thus the continents) apart. As the magma cools, it forms new crust. Where plates collide, new mountain ranges are sometimes created.

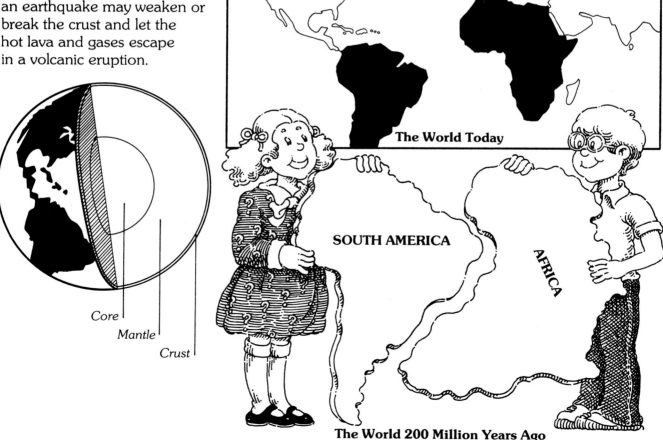

The World Today

SOUTH AMERICA

AFRICA

The World 200 Million Years Ago

Riverside Geyser, Yellowstone National Park

Why are the geysers in Yellowstone National Park so hot?

Yellowstone National Park is famous for its geysers and hot springs. Parts of the park are thought to be on top of a large, underground pool of hot, probably melted rock. The pool may be 155 miles deep, and the melted rock in it may have risen from 3000 miles inside the earth! The hot rocks heat the water in the springs and geysers.

A MAMMAL THAT LAYS EGGS...!!!

The most unusual mammal in Australia—and maybe in the whole world—is the duck-billed platypus. It has a bill that looks like a duck's, sharp claws on webbed feet, and a tail that is flat like a beaver's. The males have a poison spur on each of their hind feet. When a platypus skin was first shown in England, in 1798, people thought it was a fake made from pieces taken from other animals!

Probably the strangest thing about the platypus is that it lays eggs. And the eggs this one-to two-foot-long mammal lays are no bigger than a sparrow's! The eggs are a little like reptiles' eggs—they have a tough, rubbery shell. The female usually lays two eggs at a time in a nest of leaves and grass built inside a long, twisting burrow. She keeps them next to her warm body until they hatch, usually in ten to twelve days.

Duck-billed platypuses live only in Australia. That is probably because ages and ages ago the Australian continent drifted away from the other continents. It has been by itself in the Pacific Ocean for about 25 million years.

Because Australia has been isolated, the wild animals living there evolved in different ways than the animals on other continents. Duck-billed platypuses apparently came into existence in Australia and never went to other continents because they couldn't swim across the wide Pacific Ocean.

What is an earthquake?

An earthquake is a sudden motion inside the earth that shakes the earth's surface. According to some seismologists (size-MOL-o-jists), earthquake scientists, even tremors so slight that only sensitive instruments can measure them are called earthquakes.

What causes earthquakes?

Strictly speaking, anything that makes the earth shake or vibrate. That includes trucks rumbling down the highway and underground atomic blasts. Volcanoes sometimes cause earthquakes.

But the big earthquakes we all think about, such as the one that killed more than 1,500 people in Rumania in 1975 (see photo), result from the splitting and shifting of underground rock under pressure. This splitting usually begins from 11 to 21 miles below the earth's surface, though it sometimes begins even deeper.

What causes underground rocks to split?

Underground rock splits because of the pressure put on it by the movement of the huge plates of rock that make up the earth's crust. These plates lie on top of the mantle, the layer of rock between the crust and the extremely hot core. The plates can move because the part of the mantle closest to the plates is made up of melted rock that lets the plates slide across it. Hot lava flowing up through the spaces between the plates pushes the plates

Earthquake damage in Bucharest. Rumania. 1975

apart. Some of the plates slide against each other in opposite directions. That often happens along the San Andreas fault in California (see photo below). Some plates slide underneath others, creating deep trenches. When the plates move, they put strain on the rocks in the crust. Sometimes the strain is too much and the rocks break, creating earthquakes.

San Andreas Fault. California

ANIMALS MAY BE ABLE TO PREDICT EARTHQUAKES!

All through history there have been stories of animals doing odd things just before earthquakes. Weasels, mice, and moles have been seen rushing out of their burrows. Great flocks of sea birds have flown far inland. Large numbers of rats have appeared suddenly. Pandas have made strange screaming sounds. Hibernating snakes have crawled out of their holes and frozen to death. Shrimps have crawled onto dry land. Some kinds of fish that live on the bottoms of rivers and lakes have been seen leaping out of the water again and again.

Scientists all around the world are trying to figure out what all this odd animal behavior means. Maybe some animals can feel the ground tremble a tiny bit before we do. Maybe they hear sounds coming from inside the earth that humans can't hear. Or perhaps they smell gases pushed from the soil by rocks that are moving far underground.

If scientists can find out what animals are sensing, they might be able to build instruments that could detect the same signals. Then people could be told beforehand that an earthquake is coming and they could go to a safe place.

In the meantime, scientists are watching closely when animals start acting strangely. In China, in 1975, animals helped scientists to predict an earthquake. Nearly a million people left their homes a few hours ahead of the earthquake. The quake destroyed their city, but they were safe.

Where do tidal waves come from?

What people *call* tidal waves aren't really caused by the tides. They're caused by underwater volcanic explosions, earthquakes, or landslides that shake the ocean floor and move the water above it. Giant waves then flash through the water at jet-plane speeds—about 450 miles per hour!

Another name for tidal waves is *tsunami* (tsoo-NA-mee), a Japanese word that means "large waves in the harbor." And that's where they do their damage. While far out at sea, the tsunami are long and low and can pass beneath a ship without so much as a bounce. But when they reach a shallow area they can rise as high as a 10-story building before crashing onto shore.

Most tsunami happen in the Pacific Ocean, where there are lots of volcanoes and earthquakes. Japan has been hit by about 150 disastrous tsunami since record keeping began. But thanks to a modern radio warning system, today people can reach safe places in the hills before the killer waves hit.

Is it true that some rocks can float on water?

Yes. A rock named *pumice* sometimes floats. It forms when red-hot liquid rock (lava) flows out of erupting volcanoes and cools very rapidly. Bubbles of gas and air are trapped in the liquid rock. When it cools and hardens, these bubbles leave tiny holes all through the rock. If there are many, many holes, the pumice is light enough to float. If there are very few holes, the pumice sinks in water.

The bubbles in pumice make it the lightest stone in the world. Some history books tell how sailors were saved after the Krakatoa volcano erupted in Indonesia in 1883. They walked two miles from their ship to the shore on a thick floating carpet of piled up pumice!

What are rocks made of?

Rocks are made mostly of minerals, such as salt and quartz. Some rocks are made up of only one mineral. Other rocks are made up of two or three minerals mixed together. Some rocks are made of minerals mixed with other materials.

Minerals are usually in the form of crystals. Crystals are often shiny and you can see some of their straight edges and sharp corners. However, some crystals are so small they can't be seen, even through a microscope.

Minerals have many qualities. Some minerals are elastic and return to their original shape after they are bent. Others are very hard and can be used to cut other minerals.

Mineral crystals can break apart. Later they may join with other minerals to form new rocks. It takes many years, even millions, for rocks to form because minerals break apart and join together very slowly.

What holds mineral crystals together? Sometimes they join like the pieces of a jigsaw puzzle. They may also be pressed, cemented, squeezed, or melted together.

When does a hill become a mountain?

Topographers (toe-POG-ra-phers), scientists who study the surface of the earth, usually agree that when a hill is 2000 feet higher than the land around it, it may be called a mountain.

Of course, the word "mountain" means different things to different people. Those who live in a plains area might call a 500-foot hill a "mountain." In a place like Colorado, it would be considered just a bump on the ground!

The tallest mountain in the world is Mount Everest, which is 29,028 feet high. It is in the Himalayan Mountains between Nepal and Tibet.

SOME ISLANDS ARE MADE OF SKELETONS!

Coral reefs and islands may look as if they are made of rocks, but they're not! They are formed from millions of skeletons that once were the outer covering of small sea animals called *polyps.*

Most coral polyps are yellow, brown, or olive green, but their skeletons are always white.

Coral polyps secrete their skeletons from special cells at their bases. These round skeletons are hard and protect the delicate polyps inside. When coral polyps die, their skeletons remain.

New polyps grow on the skeletons left behind by polyps that have died. After many years, great mounds of coral form. The mounds grow so slowly

Coral polyps

Skeletons of coral polyps

that it has taken over 25 million years to build the Great Barrier Reef. This coral reef, off the northeastern coast of Australia, is one of the wonders of the world. It is about 1,250 miles long and covers an area the size of Kansas. Over 350 kinds of coral are found in this reef.

Plants called stony seaweeds also help build reefs. They take minerals from the water and form stony layers on top of the coral skeletons. Sand and the shells of tiny sea creatures fill in the open spots on the reef and build it even higher.

The mounds of coral and sand grow until they reach the surface of the sea. Sometimes sand gathers on top of the reef. In time it forms a small island.

Coral island in the South Pacific Ocean

You got me!

How was Devils Tower made?

Hot, melted rock from deep inside the earth created the famous Devils Tower, an unusual rock formation in northeastern Wyoming.

Ages ago melted rock pushed up through a crack in the earth's crust. As the soft rock neared the surface, it cooled. The cooling rock shrank and separated into tall columns as it hardened.

At one time the tower was covered by softer rock and soil. Over the ages, wind and water wore the soft land away, but could not erode the hard rock of the tower. Now it stands 865 feet above its tree-covered base and 1,280 feet above the Belle Fourche (Foosh) River, which probably did most of the eroding. The Tower and its base are 30 feet higher than the Empire State Building.

How are sand dunes formed?

As sand is blown along by the wind, some of the grains of sand drop around small objects: rocks or bushes or fences. As more sand collects around the object, a small hill begins to form. Wind continues to push sand up the gentle slope of the windward side (the side where the wind first hits), then drops it over the crest onto the steeper lee slope (the side facing away from the wind). Before long, the little hill has grown into a large dune. As the dune grows, it moves across land. Why? The wind carries sand *from* the windward side *to* the leeward side of the dune.

Deserts like the Sahara have chains of dunes 100 miles long.

Is sand really ground up rocks?

Sand is different on different beaches.

Most sand is made from rocks, but some of it comes from the skeletons of tiny sea animals.

New England sand is mainly crystals of quartz rock. This sand was made during the Ice Ages by glaciers grinding through the eastern mountains.

In the warm seas of southern Florida, sand comes mostly from limestone—rock formed from bits of seashells, coral, and other remains from the bodies of dead marine animals.

California sand may be light, powdery rock which has been worn away from seashore cliffs by the action of waves.

Many beaches in Oregon and Washington are made of fine-grained, green-gray sand. This sand came from molten rock that seeped from the earth ages ago.

In Hawaii some beaches are white or pink coral sand. Other beaches are dark brown or gray; their sand comes from the lava and ashes of volcanoes.

Certain beaches in Australia are made of "star sand." Each grain of sand is a tiny star, the skeleton of a one-celled animal known as a *foram*.

DON'T LET QUICKSAND TRAP YOU

Quicksand is a bed of ordinary sand floating on water that is slowly moving upward from an underground spring. Even though the water moves slowly, it pushes upward enough to lift the grains of sand slightly and make them "quick," or moving.

Quicksand will not suck you down! In fact, it has a *lifting* effect. Scientists agree that quicksand will support more weight than water alone. You can *even float* in it just as you can float in a swimming pool.

If you get caught in quicksand, don't struggle. Struggling could make you lose your balance and cause you to drown. Carefully take off any load you are carrying, such as a knapsack. Try to throw it out of the quicksand area.

Next, fall backward gently in a spread-eagle position just as if you were floating on your back in water. Then free your legs slowly, one at a time, and squirm or swim to firm ground.

How is petrified wood formed?

In general, petrified wood is formed like this: a fallen-down tree or broken branch gets buried in mud, sand, or even volcanic ash for many thousands of years. Water or other moisture slowly seeps into the wood. The water contains minerals which fill the cells of the wood and harden, often *in the exact shape of the cell.* The wood eventually rots away. What is left is a perfect copy of the wood, in stone. It is a *fossil* of the tree or branch.

So, petrified "wood" is really stone. The colors in the stone are caused by various chemicals in the water.

Why is the sky blue?

When it leaves the sun, light is a mixture of several colors—including red, yellow, blue, and violet. But when this mixture hits the earth's atmosphere, something fascinating happens. The red and yellow parts of the light pass right through the atmosphere in a fairly straight path. But the blue and violet light gets bounced around and scattered by the molecules of air. It's as if you tried to run in a straight line through a roomful of people—you'd bump into some of them.

So, on earth the sun usually looks yellow because the yellow light seldom bumps into molecules in the air. It comes to our eyes almost directly from the sun. But because the blue and violet light has been bounced around, it approaches us from all directions. That makes the sky look blue.

What makes the wind blow?

The weight of air is not always the same. Air is made up of tiny, invisible particles of gas. When air is warmed, the tiny particles spread away from one another. When air is cooled, the particles come closer together. Warm air is light and does not press down heavily on the earth. Cool air is heavier and moves in to take the place of warm air, which rises. This movement of air is what we call the wind.

Why is some air warmer and some air cooler? The sun warms all the air, of course. But the sun heats land faster than it heats water. During the day, the air above land is warmer and therefore lighter than it is above seas and lakes. So by day the wind usually blows from the water toward the land.

The opposite can happen at night. Even though water heats more slowly than land under the sun's rays, it keeps its heat longer. At night the air over land becomes cooler and heavier than the air over water. So the wind changes and blows from land toward water.

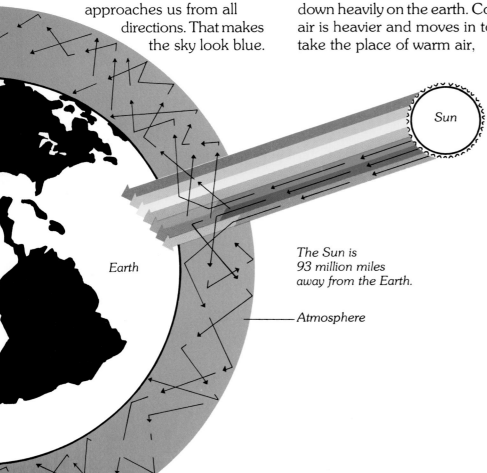

The Sun is 93 million miles away from the Earth.

Earth

Sun

Atmosphere

Does the sky ever end?

Yes, if you think of the sky as the covering of air that surrounds the world. That covering is called the atmosphere, and there is less and less of it the higher you go. Ninety-nine percent of all air is found below an imaginary line about 30 miles above the earth.

What keeps the air from floating off into space?

The same thing that holds us on the earth—the pull of gravity. Gravity gives weight to air and keeps it in a blanket around the earth. That blanket of air is the atmosphere. Without gravity, we wouldn't have air to breathe!

What is a hurricane?

Hurricanes are powerful storms that start over tropical oceans. To be called a hurricane, a storm must have winds that blow at least 75 miles (120 km) per hour.

Hurricane winds and rain clouds whirl around an *eye,* or calm area, in the center of the storm. Surrounding the *eye* is a wall of storm clouds that have the strongest winds in the hurricane. These winds may blow 150 miles (240 km) per hour. They can tear up full-grown trees and create huge waves. Cities in the paths of hurricanes are sometimes badly damaged.

Hurricanes get much of their energy from warm, moist air that rises, cools, and releases rain. When a hurricane travels over land or cooler water, it usually dies down because it doesn't have the warm, moist air it needs to continue.

A RACE BETWEEN THUNDER AND LIGHTNING!

Lightning and thunder begin almost at the same time. But you *see* the flash before you *hear* the noise! This happens because light travels much faster than sound. Light travels so fast that you see it almost instantly—even if it's far away. But it takes 5 seconds for the sound of thunder from a storm 1 mile away to travel to your ear.

So, if you *see* lightning, listen for thunder. As soon as you *see* a bolt of lightning, start counting seconds— "*one elephant, two elephants,*" and so on. At a normal pace it takes about 1 second to say "*one elephant,*" 5 seconds to count to "*five elephants.*" (Lightning can be dangerous,

so count inside your house or some other safe shelter.)

Just remember—it takes 5 seconds for thunder to go 1 mile. So if the time between seeing a lightning flash and hearing the thunder is 5 seconds, the thunderstorm is 1 mile away. If the time is 10 seconds, the storm is 2 miles away. When you see lightning and hear thunder at almost the same time, the storm is right over your head!

Hurricane Betsy, Miami, Florida, 1965

IT NEVER RAINS CATS AND DOGS, *BUT . . .*

frogs and little fish have been known to fall from the sky. This happens when a tornado scoops up these animals from a pond and dumps them on dry land.

Are all raindrops the same size?

No. Raindrops begin in the clouds as tiny water droplets. Some water droplets are so small it takes 2,500 of them in a row to measure one inch. Air currents in the clouds move the droplets about, keeping the droplets from being pulled downward by the earth's gravity. But not all the droplets in the cloud are that small. Some bump into others and join together. These droplets are moved about more slowly and on different paths, so they bump into other droplets and become still larger. When they are ten times larger than the little ones, they can fall to earth. If the droplets form in a low, thin cloud that has little up-and-down air motion inside it, they will fall as a fine drizzle. If they are in a fat, tall storm cloud they will be bounced against each other until they are much larger before they fall.

Regardless of size, all raindrops are round.

18

Does a halo around the moon mean rain will come soon?

Meteorologists (me-tee-oh-RAHL-ah-jists), scientists who study weather, agree that a halo *can* mean that rain is coming. The halo is caused when moonlight hits ice crystals in thin, wispy clouds that are more than 20,000 feet above the earth. The moonlight reflects off the crystals and forms a halo. Some halos have the colors of rainbows.

High, thin clouds often move ahead of storms, so when you see a halo around the moon, you know there is a good chance that rain is on its way.

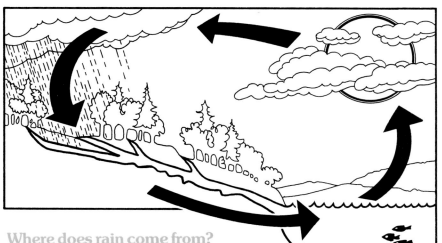

Where does rain come from?

Rain comes not from the sky but from our own very watery earth. Look at a map or globe of the world. You will see almost three times as much blue ocean as land.

The drawing above shows what really happens to water. It is called the *hydrological* (HIGH-dro-LOJ-i-cal) cycle, which means "water wheel." Part of that cycle we see as falling rain—or hail or snow. But we do not see the upward journey of water.

The upward journey of water starts when the sun heats the surface of the oceans and other bodies of water. Some of the water becomes an invisible gas called water vapor. When water turns from a liquid to a gas, we say it *evaporates.*

The water vapor mixes with other gases in the air and is carried upward and cooled. As it cools, it *condenses*—forms water droplets—on bits of ice high in the air. These droplets of water form clouds. The droplets in the clouds bump into each other and join to form larger drops. When they are too heavy to be held up by air, gravity pulls them to earth as rain.

Much of the rain that falls seeps into streams which run into rivers that flow into seas. And always, from the surface of the sea and other bodies of water, from the moist parts of the earth, from the leaves of plants and the breath of animals, water is returning to the air as water vapor. Clouds form, and the rain cycle starts all over again.

Does dew fall from fog?

No. Dew doesn't fall. Dew forms when water vapor in warm air touches a cold object. The cold makes the water vapor *condense*, or form small water drops. This usually happens on clear nights when the ground cools off. The ground and the plants growing on it become cooler than the air, so the water vapor in the air condenses on the plants. Insects like the dragonfly below sometimes become covered with dew. Then they wait for the sun to warm them and dry their wings so they can fly away.

Why does some rain taste bitter?

It may taste bitter because the raindrops contain acids. "Acid rain" is created when rain mixes with pollution in the air. In cities, acid rain can damage marble buildings and statues. In rivers and lakes it can kill fish eggs, and on land it can damage soil needed for the proper growth of plants.

What causes the mists above ponds and lakes?

That kind of mist is sometimes called *steam fog*. It may be seen on cold winter mornings and on clear summer nights when there is a big difference between the temperature of the water and that of the air above it. The water must be much warmer than the air. Warm water evaporates (changes into a gas called water vapor) faster than cold water does. Cold air can hold less water vapor than warm air can. The warmer water of the lake is evaporating fast and the colder air above it cannot hold all the water vapor. So some of the water vapor condenses (changes back into a cloud of water droplets) almost as soon as it hits the cold air.

What makes rainbows?

Rainbows form because sunlight is a mixture of many colors. When a ray of sunlight shines at a certain angle on raindrops, the raindrops act as prisms. The raindrops separate the light into bands of red, orange, yellow, green, blue, indigo, and violet, and reflect the bands back to earth in the form of a rainbow.

Do oceans ever freeze?

Except for the Arctic and Antarctic oceans, most oceans never get cold enough to freeze. Currents of warm water from oceans where it is summertime are always being carried to the oceans where it is wintertime. The oceans' rolling waves and swells also help to keep them from freezing. Then, too, salt water has a lower freezing point (temperature at which it turns to ice) than fresh water.

Why are there ocean waves when there is no wind?

The wind starts *most* waves, but not all of them. Sometimes a sudden movement on the ocean floor will cause waves to form. Underwater landslides, earthquakes, or volcanoes can send huge, dangerous waves traveling across the ocean. The sun and the moon also pull at the oceans. This pull makes the water rise and fall, causing high and low tides.

But most waves *are* caused by stormy winds blowing across the ocean's surface. That is true even of ordinary size waves. Sometimes waves will travel thousands of miles from where they first get a push from the wind. That's why you can always see waves at the shore, even when it's not windy.

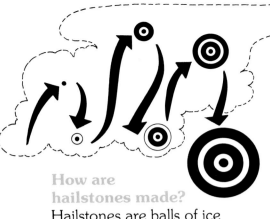

How are hailstones made?

Hailstones are balls of ice that fall from storm clouds. They may be smaller than apple seeds or as big as grapefruit. An extra large one discovered in Kansas in 1970 holds the record. It was 17.5 inches (44.5 cm) around and weighed 1.7 pounds (0.76 kg)!

All hailstones are formed in the dark, cumulonimbus (kume-yah-lo-NIM-bus) clouds of thunderstorms. In the clouds are tiny balls of ice and supercooled water—droplets of water that are liquid even though they are below freezing temperature.

Violent winds within the clouds carry some of the tiny ice balls through the supercooled water. When an ice ball hits the supercooled water, the water freezes around it and adds a new, thin layer of ice. Every time the growing hailstone is hurled up and down by the wind it gains another thin layer of ice.

When the hailstone finally becomes too heavy to be held up in the cloud by the wind, it falls to the ground.

What is a waterspout?

A waterspout is a tornado occurring over a lake or sea.

Winds make waterspouts. Spinning close to the surface of water, the winds pull water vapor (but not water itself), mist, and sea spray to form a wobbling column that looks like a snake balancing on its tail. When the winds die down, the spout disappears.

Waterspouts can be very dangerous. The winds in the walls of the funnels have reached speeds of 500 miles (800 km) per hour. Occasionally they have been strong enough to badly damage ships.

Some waterspouts are tall and skinny, others are short and stubby. The tallest waterspout ever recorded was seen offshore from New South Wales, Australia. It was over 5,014 feet (1,500 m) high—nearly a mile above the sea! Its funnel was only 10 feet (3 m) wide.

SOME ANIMALS CAN PREDICT WEATHER

Mice, frogs, and turtles are more active in the 24-hour period before a storm. Deer and songbirds feed heavily before storms arrive.

Swallows are sometimes called "storm swallows" or "rain swallows." They zoom through the air hunting tiny insects—and when insects fly low, so do the swallows. When swallows fly low, rain is coming. When they fly high, sunny weather will continue.

Insects probably fly low before a rainstorm because the extra moisture in the air makes their wings damp and heavy. That could also explain the origin of the folk saying: "When bees stop buzzing, rain is coming."

Are there still glaciers anywhere on earth?

Yes. There are even some in the United States, and not just in Alaska.

Glaciers are rivers and seas of slowly moving ice. They can form wherever it is cold enough for snow to pile up and last from year to year. When snow becomes about 100 feet deep, the weight of the snow on top packs the snow on the bottom into solid ice. That weight also pushes the ice down the slope of the land beneath it.

Continental glaciers, the largest kind, are more like seas than rivers. The world's largest is the South Polar Ice Cap. It contains about 90 percent of the world's ice.

Parts of the edge of this glacier stick out over the water. These parts are called *ice shelves.* The rise and fall of tides crack the shelves, and flattopped icebergs break off. Some of those icebergs are over 50 miles long and 1,000 feet deep.

Valley glaciers are rivers of ice that flow very slowly down valleys of snow-capped mountains. They are smaller than continental glaciers,

but there are many more of them. The people in Seattle, Washington, and Portland, Oregon, live within sight of valley glaciers.

Some valley glaciers, like those in Washington and Oregon, melt as they move down from the cold mountaintops. Others slide all the way to the ocean, where huge chunks break off and float away as icebergs.

How big are icebergs?

Some icebergs are no more than 30 to 40 feet across. Others are many miles wide. One iceberg stood almost 550 feet above the water—nearly twice as high as the Statue of Liberty! Yet the top is just a small part of the whole iceberg. Only from 1/8th to 1/10th of an iceberg sticks out of the water. The rest of it is hidden in the sea.

Is snow always white?

No. Snow can be several colors—pink, blue, green, and even purple. Colored snow almost always appears in regions near the Arctic Circle and on glaciers. Snow turns blue when blue ice-worms live in it. That is quite unusual. The other colors are caused by algae that grow on snow under certain conditions.

ICE BEARS

Way up North in the Arctic live the white polar bears, sometimes called *ice bears.*

Most of the time, polar bears feed on seals. They need a lot of food for their 650- to 1,000-pound bodies. When hunting, a bear may lie near a seal's breathing hole in the ice and wait for the seal to come up for air. Sometimes a polar bear swims out to a piece of floating ice on which a seal is resting. With a quick *SLAM!* the bear hits the ice with its body and grabs the seal as it slides into the water.

How do bears survive the bitter cold of the Arctic? They dig their dens in snowbanks. Snow holds in heat so well that the temperature inside a den may be 40° warmer than the temperature outside. Also, these bears are well insulated. Their fur is thick and keeps their skin dry. Under their skin is a layer of fat that helps keep them warm.

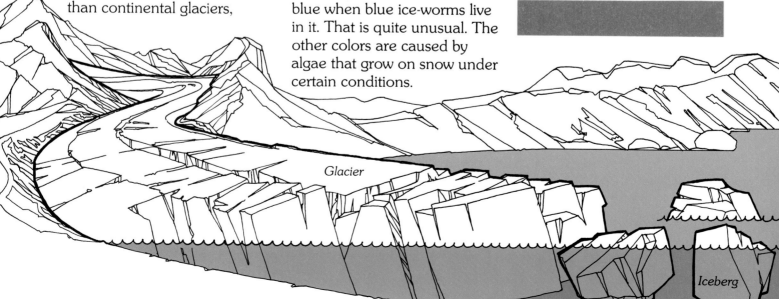

Glacier

Iceberg

How long can seeds live?

Seeds with hard coats (outer coverings) often can stay dormant (alive, but not growing) for years and years. The record length of dormancy is held by a type of lotus plant. A seed that had been picked from one of these plants in 1703 was planted 237 years later, in 1940. The seed grew! But that was not the oldest seed. Some dormant Oriental lotus seeds dug up in Japan turned out to be about 3,000 years old! And yes, some of them sprouted when scientists grew them.

How did the touch-me-not get its name?

The touch-me-not got its name because it goes **pop** when it is touched. The plant's seed pods are made of five narrow strips that grow tighter and tighter over the seeds inside. When the seeds are ripe, the strips explode at the slightest touch and flip seeds for several feet in all directions.

Why aren't there more saguaro cacti in the desert?

A mature saguaro (sah-WAH-ro) cactus produces at least 100 fruits a year, with some 2,000 seeds in each fruit. In 100 years a saguaro can produce more than 20 million seeds. So, why aren't there more saguaros? Because ants can carry away 1,000 seeds in an hour. The ants like to eat the seeds. Birds and rodents also eat saguaro seeds. Some seeds fall on rocks or places where they can't grow. Those seeds that do manage to sprout are often attacked by cutworm larvae and other enemies. Thus, only a few seeds grow to be big cacti.

What are the "parachutes" on dandelions?

The parachutes on dandelions are hairs that are modified leaves. The dandelion's big, yellow "flower" is really a bunch of *florets,* or tiny flowers. Each floret has a tuft of hair attached to a seed. When the wind catches the hairs, the hairs fly away, carrying the seeds. Where the seeds land, new dandelions may grow.

Why are cockleburs so sticky?

Cockleburs, burdocks, and sticktights have prickly seeds that help the plants spread from one place to another. Tiny hooks on the seeds stick on the fur of animals. Sooner or later, the seeds are bitten, brushed, or bumped off the animal. They fall to the ground and, if they land on a good spot, begin a new plant.

What plant has the largest seed?

The world's biggest seed is a giant coconut named the *Coco de Mer*. Coconuts are the seeds of palm trees. Coco de Mer coconuts are bigger than basketballs. Some people use them as stools! These rare coconuts grow on islands in the Indian Ocean. Hundreds of years ago, people believed that liquid drunk from a goblet made from a Coco de Mer would be free of poison. And since kings had trouble with people trying to poison them in those days, they were willing to pay thousands of dollars for a magic goblet. One fearful king traded the contents of a merchant ship for *one* Coco de Mer!

THAT'S THE BIGGEST CUP I'VE EVER "SEED"! HEE! HEE!

IT'S STRANGE, BUT TRUE!

Mexican jumping beans aren't really beans. They are seeds from arrow plants that grow in Mexico. But they really do jump. When the flowers of the arrow plants appear in spring, small moths lay eggs inside some of the young seed pods. Each egg turns into a little caterpillar that eats the seed inside the pod. Then the caterpillar lines the inside of the pod with silk.

When the seeds fall to the ground, the hot sun and sand make the caterpillars inside the seed pods jump and hop. A caterpillar grabs the silk lining with its legs and flips its body. The seed may eventually bounce to a shady spot.

Jumping beans only last about six months because the caterpillars change into pupae and escape from the seeds as moths.

Arrow plant seed

Caterpillar inside seed pod

Emerging moth

Why don't trees fall over?

Trees don't fall when the wind blows because they are anchored in the soil by roots. Tree roots wind through the soil so much that they keep both plant and soil in place.

What do roots do?

Roots hold plants in the ground. They also absorb water and minerals from the soil and start them on the way to the rest of the plant.

The big woody roots of trees aren't the roots that actually take in water and minerals. These big roots branch out into smaller and smaller ones. The very smallest roots are about one inch (2.5 cm) long and thinner than a piece of string. The growing tips of these tiny roots push through the soil. Just behind the growing tips sprout thousands and thousands of tiny root hairs. The root hairs are what absorb water and minerals from the soil. From the root hairs, water and minerals travel through the tiny roots to the bigger roots, up the trunk, and finally into the leaves.

How long are roots?

Roots can be amazingly long. Taproots go the deepest straight into the ground. A fig tree in South Africa is said to have a taproot 400 feet long. Roots that don't grow deep are very, very long. A single plant of ordinary rye grass growing in a box 2 feet high, 2 feet wide, and 2 feet deep had nearly 14 *million* roots and 14 *billion* root hairs. If you could put them end to end, the roots would make a line 387 miles long. The root hairs would make a line about 6,000 miles long!

Do all plants have the same kinds of roots?

No. Grasses have roots that look like threads bunched up together just below the surface of the soil. These *fibrous* roots soak up rain and prevent the soil from being washed away. Other plants, such as oak and walnut trees, have *taproots*. Taproots are thick and grow downward like an underground trunk. Smaller roots grow out from the taproot just as branches grow out from the trunk. Some plants have both fibrous roots and a taproot.

ASIAN LICORICE

ASIAN LICORICE

MALLOW FROM THE MARSH

ASIA

EUROPEAN MALLOWS

IMPORTED

IMPORTED

SCHANZER

LICORICE FROM EUROPE

JIM'S INCREDIBLE EDIBLES

Taproot

Candy comes from roots?
Yes! Several kinds of candy are made from the roots of plants. Take marshmallows for instance. They are named after a plant called *marsh mallow*. This plant belongs to the mallow family that grows in salt marshes, mostly in eastern Europe and northern Africa. The stalk is about six feet high and the flowers are pink.

Years ago, the roots of this plant supplied the sweet, gummy material needed for making marshmallows. Today, most marshmallows are made more cheaply from corn syrup, cornstarch, parts of eggs, gelatin, and sugar.

People who make modern marshmallows depend on corn plants for the syrup and starch and on sugar beets or sugar cane for the sugar. So even the imitation is made from plants. But the roots of the marsh mallow plant deserve credit for supplying the original ingredients.

You might not think a plant has anything to do with delicious licorice treats, but it does. Licorice candies come from a plant called *sweetroot*. Sweetroot grows in southern Europe and in parts of Asia and the United States. Its roots are made into a black paste, and that paste is used to give licorice candy its special flavor.

THE INCREDIBLE, EDIBLE ROOT

Feeling hungry? Eat a root! Anytime you eat carrots or beets, you are eating roots. Some wild animals also include roots in their diets. Wild pigs poke their snouts into the ground to gobble up roots. Marsh rabbits and nutria dig up roots to eat. So do some mice and moles.

A root lover known to many people is the muskrat. About the size of housecats, muskrats live near marshes, ponds, and slow streams. They dig dens in banks and build domed houses out of water plants. Their favorite food is roots, especially those of cattails, arrowhead, water lillies, and bulrushes. Muskrats swim to the bottom of the water, pull up pawfulls of roots, and carry them home to nibble in safety.

Fibrous root

29

Why do plants have leaves?

Leaves are very important because they take carbon, hydrogen, and oxygen from the air and water and make them into sugar—the food of life. This process is called *photosynthesis,* and it begins when sunlight hits a green leaf. Photosynthesis makes oxygen for us to breathe as well as food for us to eat. Inside the leaves are tiny cells called *chloroplasts.* Chloroplasts contain *chlorophyll* (KLOR-oh-fill), the green pigment that makes it possible for leaves to use sunlight to make sugar.

Where does the color in autumn leaves come from?

Each leaf is made up of thousands of tiny cells. Inside each cell are colored chemicals—green, yellow, and brown. In summer, the green chemical, chlorophyll, uses sunlight and water to make sugar to feed the tree. Chlorophyll hides the yellow and

I know!

brown of the other chemicals.

Towards winter, a corky layer forms where the leaf joins the twig. This layer cuts off the tiny pipelines that carry water and food to and from the leaf.

When the pipelines are closed, some chlorophyll

is left in the leaves. On sunny days, this chlorophyll is made into sugar. Then the yellow and brown chemicals that have really been there all the time can be seen.

The sugar made from the remaining chlorophyll combines with other chemicals in the leaf and turns it red or purple.

When is a tree not a tree?

A tree is not a tree when it's a banana plant! Banana plants look like trees because they have big thick "trunks" and long green leaves at the top. But they aren't trees because their "trunks" aren't made of wood.

The banana is a gigantic

herb, the biggest plant on earth without a woody stem. What appears to be a hard trunk is actually soft banana leaves wrapped tightly around one another like the stalks of a bunch of celery.

Which evergreen tree has the longest needles?

The longleaf pine of the southeastern United States. The needles grow as long as 18 inches (45 cm), usually in bundles of three. People collect them, tie them in bunches, and use them as brooms.

How did the "dandelion" get its name?

Dandelion leaves look like the teeth of a lion—or so people thought long ago. In France these plants were called *dent de lion* (tooth of the lion). From that name we get the word *dandelion*.

HOME SWEET HOME

Imagine being able to camp out without lugging along a sleeping bag or a tent. Leaf-rolling grasshoppers, which live in the southeastern part of the United States, do just that! They can stop anyplace they want and make a shelter out of leaves to protect themselves from enemies or bad weather.

Every night, leaf-rolling grasshoppers hunt aphids, their favorite food. And every day, they build new shelters out of leaves. For one of these grasshoppers, it's easy. The grasshopper just rolls a leaf around itself and then sews the edges of the leaf together with silk it secretes from special glands.

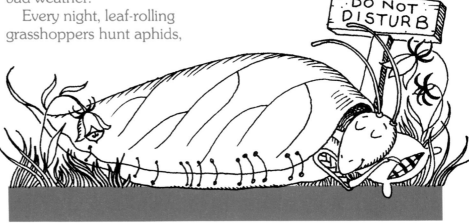

How many kinds of trees are there in the United States?

There are over 1,000 kinds of trees in the United States.

Trees are divided into three main groups. The largest group is the broad-leaved trees. Most of these are deciduous (dee-SIJ-you-us) trees, which means they shed their leaves in late fall.

Next are the conifers (KON-uh-fers) or cone-bearing trees. Conifers have green leaves, or needles, the year round. That is why they are sometimes called *evergreens*.

The third and the smallest group of trees is the palms. Palm trees don't have branches, and the leaves all come out of the top of the tree.

What trees live longest?

The oldest trees in the world are bristlecone pines. These twisted, gnarled trees live high in the White Mountains of California. They grow slowly—as little as 40 feet in 4,000 years! The most ancient bristlecone pine ever known was 4,600 years old when it was cut down. This tree had already been alive 2,500 years when the Roman Empire was founded. You can see these trees in a section of the Inyo National Forest.

Why don't maple trees die when their sap is taken?

When sugar maple trees are tapped in the spring, up to four spiles (spouts) are put in each tree. Each spile drains sap from a small part of the sap-carrying layer *(sapwood)*. The sap contains food and water. The tree can afford to lose a small amount of sap, but if the sapwood were cut through all the way around the tree, the tree would starve.

Are all the parts of a live tree alive?

No. The outer layer of the bark is dead. Also, most of the wood in the trunk and branches (the heartwood) is dead except for some thin layers just inside the bark. One of these layers (the cambium) forms new cells that become tiny tubes for carrying water and minerals. The leaves are also alive.

What is the biggest tree?

Giant sequoias (se-QWOI-ahs) are the *biggest* trees in the world. The largest sequoia, named *General Sherman,* is estimated to weigh over 2,000 tons. It is 272 feet tall and measures 79 feet around its trunk. You can see General Sherman and other giant sequoias growing in Sequoia National Park in California.

The *tallest* trees are California redwoods. They grow to be more than 300 feet high—about the height of a thirty-story building.

Heartwood

Sapwood

Cambium

Bark

The General Sherman sequoia

THE *ORIGINAL* APARTMENT HOUSE

Did you know that an old hollow tree is a lot like an apartment house in the middle of a big city? If you look at the top of the tree, you will notice a real wildlife penthouse! Woodpeckers, chickadees, bluebirds, and tree swallows make their dry, cozy, fly-in homes there.

The balcony apartments are the nests out on the limbs that are still alive. Built by hummingbirds, Northern orioles, and many other birds, these nests are used mostly for raising families in the spring and summer months.

The second story walk-up is a large hole. It is often used by raccoons. The strong "walls" of the tree keep out the winds and rain.

Many other animals also live in the walk-up apartments. Opossums, fishers, squirrels, even bobcats love to make their homes in an empty hollow tree.

The basement apartments are also popular. Chipmunks tunnel under the roots and dig rooms for storing food and sleeping. The roots serve as strong bars that keep out bigger enemies. Skunks, weasels, rabbits, and woodchucks also like basement apartments.

Should everyone buy live Christmas Trees?

Buying live Christmas trees is a great idea. But for people who have no place to plant a tree, regular Christmas trees are just fine. Cutting them doesn't really disturb our forests because many Christmas trees are grown on special Christmas-tree farms. The trees on these farms are planted, cultivated, pruned, and cut just for the holidays. Usually, these trees are cut when they are about 10 years old and 4 to 6 feet tall.

Does moss really grow only on the north side of trees?

No. Moss often grows on the north side of trees because that is the shaded side. Moss dries out and dies in direct sunlight. But in dark, moist forests, moss grows all around the trunks of trees.

How did "nurse" logs get their name?

Nurse logs got their name from the way they nurse along seedlings. When a tree falls and begins to rot, mosses, wild flowers, and new trees grow on it. In fact, some trees—like Sitka spruce and western hemlock—can start to grow better on a log than in mineral soil. The rotting

RINGS, RINGS, RINGS

Lots of people don't like to tell other people how old they are. But trees, turtles, even some fish can't hide their age.

Each spring and summer a tree adds a new layer of wood to its trunk. The layer formed in spring grows fast and is light colored because it is made up of large cells. In summer, growth is slower. The layer formed then has smaller cells and makes a dark ring. Counting the dark rings on a tree stump tells its age.

The bony shells of turtles are covered with thin plates called *scutes*. If you want to learn about how old a box turtle is, count the number of ridges on one of its scutes.

Fish can't keep their age a secret either. Not all fish have scales, but those that do tell everyone how old they are. Every year, each scale gets a new growth ring.

Trees growing on nurse log

wood of the dead tree serves as a sort of hothouse: it holds moisture and stays warm, "nursing" the tender seedlings.

Eventually the nurse log rots completely, but its place is still marked. The trees that sprouted on it now stand in a straight line. There may be three or four trees, or twenty or more, depending on how large the nurse log was. Sooner or later, these trees fall and may become nurse logs themselves.

Have you ever seen a tree that has knees?

You have if you've ever seen a bald cypress tree. These trees have bark-covered "knees" that grow upward out of long, shallow roots that spread out from the tree.

Cypress knees often grow as tall as a man. Some are wider at their bases than a telephone pole.

No one knows for sure what the knees do. Some botanists believe that they help the tree breathe. The roots of a cypress tree grow in soft, wet soil that contains very little oxygen. The knees may take in air for the roots.

Other botanists think the cypress knees help anchor the tree. The roots are wide-spreading, but they do not grow deep enough to reach solid earth. Perhaps the knees act as a balance and help support the tall tree. Cypress trees may grow as high as 200 feet.

Bald cypress trees grow on land or in swamps and marshes from Maryland to Florida and all along the Gulf of Mexico.

Will plants grow better if you talk to them?

Probably not. No one has proved that talking to plants does them any good at all. Plants can't even hear you.

On the other hand, it probably won't hurt your African violets or geraniums to tell them how much you love them or, if you prefer, even to sing them a little song. Of course, your friends may think you've gone crazy.

What is pollen?

Pollen grains are the tiny yellow specks of dust inside most flowers. Each pollen grain has a special shape—smooth, wrinkled, bumpy. But in any one kind of plant all the pollen grains look alike.

Pollen grows in little sacks in the anthers (male parts) of flowers. For seeds to form, pollen must reach the stigmas (female parts) of flowers. When the pollen is deposited on a stigma, the flower is pollinated and seeds develop.

As plants can't walk around, they need help pollinating their flowers. The showy colors, nectar, and sweet perfume of many flowers attract insects for this purpose. Pollen sticks to the insects, and they carry it from plant to plant.

Many plants are pollinated by the wind. These plants—the grasses and many trees—have dull, odorless flowers. But they make lots and lots of pollen grains. A few grains are blown onto the stigma of another flower of its kind, and the process that creates new seeds begins once again.

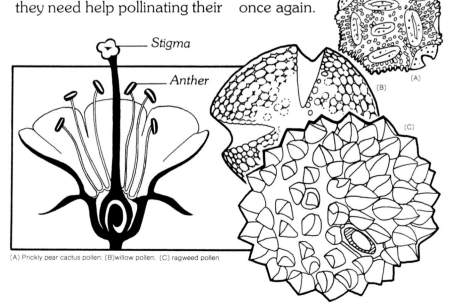

— Stigma

— Anther

(A) Prickly pear cactus pollen; (B) willow pollen; (C) ragweed pollen

Do people eat grass?

Yes. You can't actually sit on a lawn and eat grass because your stomach can't digest plant material. But much of the food you eat comes from grass. Bread is made from flour, which is made by grinding the seeds of grasses. The seeds of wheat and rye are the grains most commonly used to make bread, but the seeds of corn, rice, oats, barley, and millet are also made into bread and cereals. Much sugar is refined from juices taken

Pronghorn antelope grazing

from the stems of a giant grass, sugar cane.

Many animals besides human beings eat grass. Cattle, sheep, goats, and many wild animals live mostly on grass. Many meat-eating animals eat grass eaters, so their food, too, comes first from grass.

Grass has many other uses. It protects hilly pastures from erosion. It carpets lawns and parks. Animals make nests with it. It is used in making some medicines. In Asia, a giant grass—bamboo—is used to build houses and to make tools, bowls, paper, and many other useful things.

What is a butterfly bush?

A butterfly bush doesn't look like a butterfly. It got its nickname because all kinds of butterflies flutter to its flowers to sip nectar. Its scientific name is *Buddleia davidii*. There are different kinds, with lavender, purple, or white blossoms. Many people plant this bush in their gardens to attract butterflies.

Other plants also attract butterflies. Native American milkweed, which grows wild in lots and along roads, is called *butterfly weed*. Phlox, a low-growing garden plant, and lilies are also favorites with butterflies.

A MOST AMAZING STOMACH

An elk can stay alive by eating grass, but you can't. Why? Because an elk is a ruminant (ROO-meh-nent), an animal that has a four-chambered stomach that can digest grass. A few other ruminants are cows, giraffes, mountain goats, deer, moose, antelopes, and bison.

When an elk swallows slightly chewed grass, the grass goes into the *rumen* (ROO-min). The rumen stores lots of food, mixing and mashing it. Bacteria begin breaking the grass down into chemicals that provide energy and build body tissue.

The grass then goes to the *reticulum* (reh-TIC-you-lem). There it is turned into cuds, or small balls. After several hours, the elk coughs the cud up into its mouth and thoroughly chews it.

Once the cud is mushy, it is swallowed. It passes through the first two chambers and stops in the third one, the *omasum*, (oh-MAY-sum). Little is known about what happens there.

The fourth chamber, the *abomasum* (ab-oh-MAY-sum), is most like your stomach. It finishes digesting the food into a watery fluid. The fluid enters the intestine, where it is absorbed into the bloodstream. What began as grass is now fuel for the cells of the elk's body.

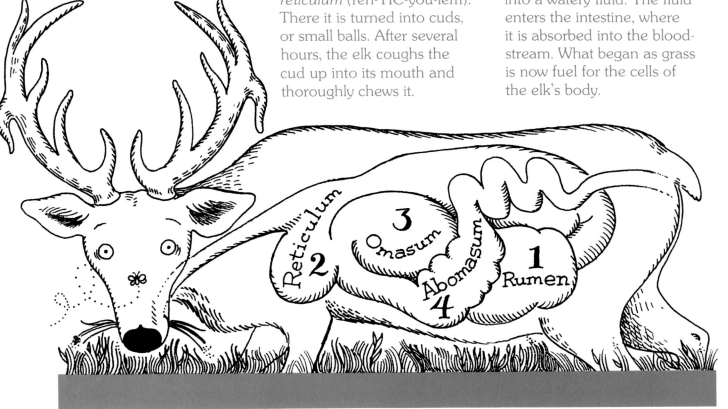

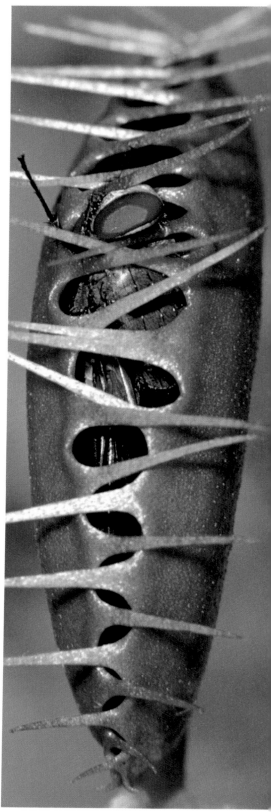

SOME PLANTS EAT BUGS FOR DINNER!!

A *few* types of plants that grow in the United States eat insects. Among these plants are the Venus's flytrap and the sundew.

The Venus's flytrap (shown on this page) grows near swamps in North Carolina. Its leaves are from three to six inches long. Each leaf has two sides, and each side has three special *trigger* hairs. If an insect touches one hair twice or two different hairs within about twenty seconds, the halves of

the leaf quickly clamp together and trap the insect. Special juices from digestive glands on the surface of the leaf digest the insect in five to ten days. The trap opens and is ready for another victim.

The sundew (shown on this page) grows in sandy bogs from Labrador to Florida and from Alaska to California. Its leaves may be round, oval, or long and thin. The top of each leaf has about 200 hairs, or *tentacles*. Each hair forms a drop of sticky fluid that attracts insects. An insect that lands on a leaf becomes stuck in the fluid. The hairs then bend over the insect and the fluid begins to digest it. What's for dessert!

Is hay fever caused by hay?

No. Hay fever isn't a fever at all. It is an irritation of the eyes and nose called an allergy. The irritation isn't caused by hay, but by pollen from trees and other plants. When people are allergic to pollen floating in the air, their bodies react: *sniffle, sniffle, ah-choo!*

Why does it hurt when you touch stinging nettle?

Stinging nettle has on its leaves and stems thousands of stiff, brittle hairs that contain a watery poison. The tip of each hair has a little round knob. Where you touch the plant, the knobs break off the hairs. The hairs pierce your skin, and the poison squirts into the wound. The wound can sting and itch, but the pain doesn't last long.

Is poison ivy safe to touch in winter?

In winter no less than in summer, the entire poison ivy plant—including its roots—is covered with an oil that easily rubs off on people's skin and clothing. This oil makes skin itch and, in some cases, blister. Also, the smoke from burning poison ivy is harmful to breathe.

If you touch poison ivy, wash the area several times with soap and running water. And don't scratch—that spreads the irritating oil!

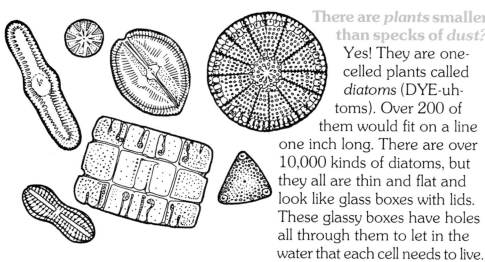

Can you live without seaweed?

Probably not, if you like ice cream. Algin, a chemical in a seaweed called kelp, is used to make ice cream creamier and to keep chocolate syrup from settling to the bottom of a glass of milk. It is also used to thicken jams, coat writing paper, and make rubber tougher. Seaweed byproducts are also added to paint, cosmetics, and medicines. And, of course, people in many countries eat seaweeds.

Prickly Pear Cactus

Why does a cactus have needles but not leaves?

First of all, many people call the sharp things on cactus plants *needles,* but they are wrong. The real name is *spine.* A cactus has spines instead of leaves because leaves lose a lot of water to the air. The water evaporates through tiny holes in the surface of each leaf. An apple tree may evaporate over ten quarts of water in one day. In the desert, where rain seldom falls, a plant with leaves would lose too much water and die. The small, non-porous spines of a cactus, along with the plant's nearly water-

There are *plants* smaller than specks of *dust?*

Yes! They are one-celled plants called *diatoms* (DYE-uh-toms). Over 200 of them would fit on a line one inch long. There are over 10,000 kinds of diatoms, but they all are thin and flat and look like glass boxes with lids. These glassy boxes have holes all through them to let in the water that each cell needs to live.

Diatoms float near the surface where sunlight can reach them. Because they are plants, they need sunlight to live. And also because they are plants, they are eaten by animals. Sea creatures as big as whales feast on millions and millions of diatoms.

A diatom reproduces by splitting in two. Each part keeps half of the outer covering and makes a new inner shell. *ONE* diatom can turn into *ONE BILLION* in *ONE MONTH!*

proof skin, prevent the cactus from losing too much of its water. A twelve-foot cactus may lose as little as two hundredths of a quart of water in a day. So, a cactus needs spines to survive in hot, dry places.

PULL THE KELP OVER YOUR SHOULDERS, DEAR, AND GO TO SLEEP . . .

That is what a mother sea otter might say to her offspring at night, if sea otters could talk. Sea otters sleep on their backs in the ocean, usually within a mile of shore. To keep from drifting farther out to sea while they are asleep, they lie beneath strands of kelp. The kelp is anchored to rocks and keeps the otters in place.

During the day, before diving for food, parents sometimes put their babies in kelp beds. That way, when the parents surface again, the youngsters will still be where the parents left them.

Sea otters aren't the only members of the ocean community that use kelp. Many kinds of creatures find shelter and food among these amazing plants that can grow two feet in one day and reach lengths of nearly 200 feet before the fronds (leaves) break off. Most important, kelp and other seaweeds make oxygen and food for all the animals in the sea.

I'm a bone-afide genius!

How do scientists figure out how to put the bones of dinosaurs together?

The scientists who put the bones of dinosaurs together have studied the bones of other dinosaurs. A few dinosaurs have been found whose skeletons are complete or nearly so. The way their bones look and the way they are connected show how the bones of other dinosaurs may fit together.

Other clues are found in the way the bones of animals living today are put together. The bones of modern animals are similar in shape, if not in size, to those of dinosaurs. The ribs of an ape, for example, look a lot like the ribs of some dinosaurs. The leg bones of chickens are almost identical in shape to the leg bones of some dinosaurs. So, by careful observation, scientists can put dinosaur bones together to make skeletons.

How do we know if a dinosaur ate meat or grass?

From just a few fossil parts of a dinosaur it is possible to figure out how big it was, how it looked, and what it ate. Fossil teeth tell the most about what a dinosaur ate.

Meat eaters would have needed long, sharp teeth to bite through the tough, armor-like skin of their victims. The tyrannosaurs had teeth 6 inches (15 cm) long. They were perfect for tearing flesh.

Grass eaters would have needed short, blunt teeth for grinding up their food. The enormous brontosaurs were about 70 feet long and weighed about 40 tons, but they had weak jaws. Their teeth were small and only strong enough to cut the soft stems of plants.

The shape of a dinosaur's body also gives scientists clues. Plant eaters often had huge, bulky bodies that held very long intestines. These intestines were needed because plant material is hard to digest and must stay in the body a long time. Meat eaters had smaller bodies.

Has anyone ever eaten meat from prehistoric animals?

Yes. About 40,000 years ago, during the Ice Age, lived huge woolly relatives of elephants called *mammoths*. A few of these became frozen in the ice. Their meat was preserved just like meat in a modern freezer. Whole mammoths have been discovered in the Arctic and people have cooked and eaten meat from them.

Can you still find dinosaur bones?

Yes indeed! The wing bones from a giant flying reptile with leathery wings longer than those on a jet fighter plane (about 50 feet) were discovered in Texas in the early 1970's.

These Texas giants are the biggest flying creatures *ever* discovered. Scientists called them *pterosaurs* (TER-ah-sores), which means "winged lizards." They lived on earth 70 million years ago, about the same time as the dinosaurs. Some scientists think pterosaurs were scavengers and ate carrion (dead animals). Their long, strong necks and stork-like jaws were useful for poking into a dead dinosaur's body.

LIVING FOSSILS

Prehistoric monsters in the movies are only make-believe. But, "living fossils" do exist. They are animals that have changed little during the history of our earth.

One such creature is the alligator, which has survived about 150 million years. Although the modern alligator is about 20 feet shorter than its ancestors, it still has the typical flat head, sharp teeth, and powerful tail.

Another living fossil is the American lobster. It looks just about the way it did 100 million years ago—complete with strong front claws and tiny, sensitive hairs that let it hear with its legs and taste with its feet.

Even that common pest, the cockroach, has been around since before dinosaurs. The cockroaches commonly found in homes will eat anything, from the food you eat to paper, clothing, and shoes. No wonder they have adapted so well to our changing world!

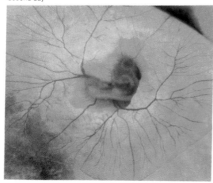
Second day

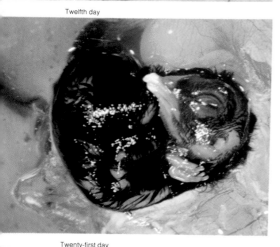
Ninth day

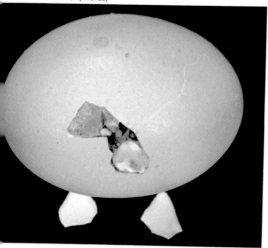
Twelfth day

Twenty-first day

How do birds grow inside eggs?

First day. A small whitish spot —the nucleus—appears after fertilization (the joining of the sperm cell from the male with the egg cell of the hen) and begins to grow.

Second day. On the second day of incubation appears a web of blood vessels carrying food to the embryo from the white and yolk. The embryo is the object shaped like a question mark in the center of the top photograph.

Ninth day. The wings, legs, and tail appear. The amniotic (am-nee-AH-tik) sac can be clearly seen. It is a colorless sac containing clear fluid which surrounds the embryo. It's sort of a swimming pool in which the embryo exercises. The little knobs on the embryo's back are where feathers will come out.

Twelfth day. The down is now visible. Also, notice the "egg tooth," the white spot on the tip of the beak. The embryo will use this "tooth" to break through the shell.

Twenty-first day. The chick breaks the shell with its egg tooth and struggles to freedom.

What birds lay the largest eggs, the smallest eggs?

The ostrich lays the world's largest egg. It's about the size of a large grapefruit, and its shell could hold about 19 chicken eggs.

The kiwi, which lives in New Zealand, lays the largest egg for its body. The egg weighs about 1 pound, which is 1/4 of the bird's weight. If an ostrich layed an egg that big, the egg would weigh over 50 pounds!

The bee hummingbird of Cuba is the smallest bird in the world and lays the smallest eggs. The bird is only 2-1/8 inches long, and its eggs are about the size of peas!

Do sharks lay eggs?

Some do. Some don't. Those that do lay eggs deposit them in a thick, rubbery case called a *mermaid's purse.* Long

threads anchor the egg case to underwater weeds or rocks.

Most sharks give live birth—from 5 to 60 babies at a time. A newborn shark is called a *pup*. Several pups born together are called a *litter*.

At birth each pup is equipped to face life on its own with a complete set of teeth.

Do crocodiles *really* eat their babies?

No. The mother crocodile below *seems* to be eating her babies, but she isn't. She is gently carrying her litter, which has just hatched, from the nest to the water. By doing that, she protects them from being eaten by hungry enemies like hawks and herons.

Crocodiles help their babies in another way. Baby crocodiles hatch out of eggs in a nest buried 8 to 12 inches under the ground. During the time between laying and the hatching, the soil on top of the eggs hardens. Sometimes the hatching babies can't dig their way out, so they yelp and croak. Their mother hears them and rips open the nest, letting the babies escape.

LIFE WITH FATHER

When people think of eggs, they probably think of hens sitting on their eggs. But mothers aren't the *only* egg-sitters. In the case of sea horses and a few other creatures, the *father* takes care of the eggs.

Male sea horses have special pouches on their bellies. At mating time, a female uses her tail to transfer 200 or more brick-red eggs into her mate's pouch. She then swims away, leaving the brooding up to him.

After the male sea horse fertilizes them, the eggs begin to grow into baby sea horses. The father's belly gets fatter and fatter. Thirty to fifty days later, papa sea horse squeezes his belly muscles. The babies squirt out, sometimes in bunches of several dozen at one time.

The young sea horses are able to care for themselves right away and begin to feed on microscopic sea creatures and plants.

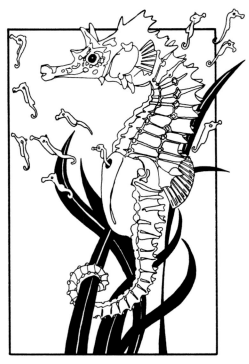

Caterpillar

Chrysalis

Adult emerging from chrysalis

Adult expanding its wings

How do caterpillars turn into moths and butterflies?

The caterpillar to the left hatched early in August from one of about 400 eggs laid on the leaves of a milkweed plant by a female monarch butterfly. After hatching, the caterpillar eats its egg case and then gorges itself on tender leaves.

As it grows bigger, the caterpillar *molts*. It forms a new skin under the old one. The old skin splits apart and the caterpillar, now larger, crawls out. The caterpillar does this four or five times in about twenty days.

About the third week after hatching, the caterpillar crawls to the underside of a branch and hangs head down, holding on with a special clasper in its tail. The skin is shed once more, and a new, hard covering called the *chrysalis* appears.

The caterpillar has now turned into a *pupa*. The pupa in the chrysalis eats no food. Instead, it lives off stored energy during the two or so weeks that it takes to emerge as an adult butterfly. To escape from the chrysalis, the new butterfly struggles enough to break the shell. After drying off in the sunshine and waiting for its wings to become firm, the bright new butterfly takes off!

Do rabbits really have lots of babies?

Yes. A healthy female cottontail rabbit could easily have 25 babies in one year. She normally has 1 to 8 offspring in a brood, with 5 being average. Many cottontail rabbits have 5 broods in one year.

How much does a baby whale weigh?

A newborn blue whale can weigh 4,000 pounds or more and be 25 feet long! It is the heaviest baby of any animal in the world. A baby elephant weighs only about 200 pounds.

Like all mammals, whale babies drink milk from their mothers. But baby whales drink while under water, and they don't have to work to get fed. Their mothers squirt the milk into their mouths! No one knows exactly how much milk baby whales drink, but scientists estimate that mother whales produce 130 quarts of milk a day. Since a baby whale nurses 40 times a day, each time it nurses it may swallow 3 or more gallons of milk!

Can one animal split and become two animals?

Yes. Planarians, worms that have flat bodies and are about the size of a matchhead, reproduce that way. At a certain stage in its life, a planarian's body begins to pinch in at the middle. The tail end holds onto something tightly as the head tries to crawl away. This tug-of-war may last for several hours. Then, suddenly, the two pull completely apart! The head end crawls away. Within a few days, it has grown a new tail and has begun feeding. Two or three weeks later it will be ready to split again.

In the meantime, the tail end stays stuck in one spot. After a few days it begins to crawl slowly about. Within a week or two it grows a new head and starts to feed and become larger. After three or four weeks it, too, is ready to reproduce again.

SO TINY, YET SO BIG

The ocean sunfish probably holds the record for the biggest increase in size from when it is born to when it is fully grown. The newly hatched fish are about one tenth of an inch long. As adults they may be ten feet long and weigh over twelve hundred pounds. This means that a baby ocean sunfish increases its weight close to sixty *million* times!

49

Who are the best animal mothers?

Mammal mothers take the greatest care of their young. At first the mothers hunt for food for their offspring. When their babies are old enough, they show them where and how to catch their own food. Mammal mothers also show their babies how to lick themselves clean. And, as their young grow up, mammal mothers try to protect them from danger.

Bird mothers probably work the hardest. Many sit on their eggs for long periods of time, day and night, and in all kinds of weather. When eggs hatch, the young have to be fed at least every half hour!

Reptile mothers are quite different. Many lay their eggs and promptly leave them forever. Some reptiles give birth to live babies and then ignore them or sometimes eat them. However, reptile babies have an advantage over mammal babies. They are "grown up" the minute they are born. A newborn poisonous snake has venom and fangs and knows how to use them.

Spider and insect mothers also have little interest in their young, except possibly to eat them. Here again, the instincts of the babies help them survive. Scorpion babies are a good example. As soon as they hatch, the babies climb onto their mother's back. They ride there until they are able to live by themselves.

THEY MUST LEARN HOW TO HUNT

Big cats are born with the instinct to hunt, but without all the necessary skills. Cheetah cubs, for example, do not know instinctively how to kill. They have to practice chasing, knocking down, and killing their prey. They acquire some skills by playing games among themselves. Later, the cubs improve their techniques and learn new ones when the mother brings live game for them to practice capturing. If the cubs fail to kill the prey after several tries, the mother kills it for them so they can see how to do it. The mother also takes the cubs on hunting trips so they can watch and imitate her.

Is it true that a bird follows the first thing it sees?

Certain birds, such as ducks, geese, quail, and cranes, follow the first moving object they see after they hatch.

Usually the first thing these chicks see is their mother. She immediately leads them to the right kind of food and to safety. But the instinct to follow right after hatching is very strong. If their parents are not close by, the young birds will follow almost anything—even a human being.

Do any animals use baby sitters?

Wolves do. In many wolf packs there are unmated "aunts" and "uncles" that take turns as "baby sitters" while the parents are away hunting. These baby-sitters often join the youngsters in their rough-and-tumble games and allow themselves to be tugged about and nipped by sharp little teeth. But there is a limit to the teasing they will take. With an angry snarl and curled lips, they warn overly pesky pups to behave themselves.

Do all predators treat their young alike?

No. When a female in a pack of wild African dogs has pups, the whole pack of up to thirty dogs stays near the den.

When the pack goes hunting, several dogs stay behind and guard the pups. Upon returning to the den, the hunters feed the pups and the guards.

Three- to four-month-old pups follow the hunters. After a kill, the pups eat first. Often not even scraps of food remain for the adults and the pack must hunt again.

In a pride of lions—a group of one to three males, several females, and cubs—the females do most of the hunting.

Sometimes females hunt as a team. But when they catch an animal, they don't share the meat. The cubs are cuffed out of the way, usually by the males, who eat first. If no food is left after the adults finish, the cubs go hungry.

Further, a female rarely bothers to take meat to the cubs still at the den. When she does try to carry food to her offspring, another adult usually steals it.

Isn't that mean of the lions?

No. Each species has proved that its way of life is successful. One species is no less admirable than the other. We can study the predators, we can admire them—but we should not judge them.

NOW, THEY'RE SUPPOSED TO BE IN BED BY 9.

THOSE AMAZING HUMANS

Ah, that's *my* kind of "mound" bar.

Why do termites build tall mounds?

The tall mounds, or *termitaries*, built by certain kinds of termites that live in tropical climates protect their inhabitants from most predators and from the heat of the sun.

The outer walls of termitaries are made from bits of soil, wood, or clay cemented together with saliva. The tallest walls are made by a kind of termite that lives in Africa and Asia. Standing up to 29 feet high, the clay walls of these mounds are so strong that it is hard to break them with a pickax. Only a few predators, such as the

THE BIGGEST NEST

The jungle fowl of Australia build the biggest nests of any birds in the world. These birds construct their nests on the ground by scraping sand and rotting leaves into a pile with their beaks and feet. Jungle fowl are only about 20 inches long, but the nests they make may be 35 feet in diameter and 15 feet high. The rotting leaves create heat inside the nests. The birds dig tunnels in the warm nests, lay their eggs in them, and then fill them up. The nests keep the eggs between 95° and 102°F, the temperature needed for hatching. After hatching, the chicks dig their way out.

aardvark to the left, can tear through the walls with their strong claws.

Termites die if they get too much heat and sun. The thick walls of the mounds keep out the sunlight. Special tunnels on the outside of the mounds let hot air out and cool air in, so the inside of the mound never gets too hot.

Is it true that gorillas live in nests?

Yes, but not the kind of nest most people are familiar with. Sitting on a strong branch, a gorilla breaks off smaller branches and twigs and stuffs them under its feet. Any little ends that stick out are tucked into the rim of the nest. All this takes only a few minutes. The gorilla works quickly and adds no frills, for it will use the simple nest for only one or two nights.

Do pack rats really steal?

Yes. These little fellows, also known as wood rats, start out with a nest of grasses, leaves, and twigs. But then they add all sorts of odds and ends—whatever they find that strikes their fancy. Shiny things attract them—bits of broken glass, buttons, eye-glasses, nails, screws, tinfoil, silverware, coins, and even brightly colored stones.

Pack rats will steal things from people's houses if they can get at them. Occasionally they leave something in return. Some naturalists think that when a pack rat finds something it likes better, it drops

whatever it is carrying to pick up the new object. That's how it got another one of its nicknames, *trade rat*.

Where do hornets get the paper to build their nests?

Hornets and wasps make their paper nests out of tiny pieces of plant fibers and wood—in much the same way that people make paper out of wood.

To make paper, the wasp chews fine splinters from bark or weathered wood. The saliva in its mouth glues the tiny pieces together into a gooey "spitball." At the nest, the wasp flattens the little ball of paper with its mouth, spreading it out into a tiny strip. After a while, there are enough strips to make a nest.

Does a spider ever get caught in its own web?

Probably not. Spiders spin their webs out of two kinds of silk. One kind is sticky enough to trap flies, but the other kind is not sticky at all. The spider walks only on the nonsticky threads. And, since spiders walk on eight "tiptoes," if one leg slipped onto the sticky threads, the spider could pull itself free with the seven other legs.

53

How do robins know where to find worms?

Some people think that robins *listen* for worms. That's what the birds seem to be doing when they turn their heads to one side. But actually they are *looking* for worms. Since robins' eyes are on the sides of their heads, they focus best to the side. They cock their heads to look for a worm poking out of its hole.

Where do penguins find fresh water to drink?

Penguins don't need fresh water at all! Sometimes they eat snow, but most of the time they just drink salt water from the ocean. They can do this because they have very large salt glands right above their nostrils. These glands remove extra salt from their blood.

Why do birds have different kinds of beaks?

Because they eat different kinds of food. Flamingos and most ducks and swans have wide bills that scoop up plants and tiny animals from the mud. Seed-eaters—like finches and cardinals—have short, fat beaks that break open hard seeds. Owls, hawks, and eagles have hooked beaks that are good for tearing flesh, and nuthatches use their thin beaks like tweezers to pick up tiny insects in bark or among leaves. The woodcock's long beak is great for jabbing into the ground for earthworms or grubs.

Bald eagle

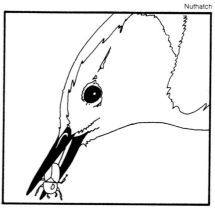

Nuthatch

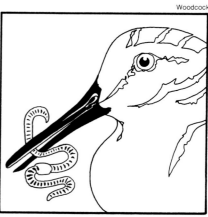

Woodcock

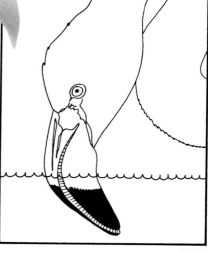

Flamingo

Cardinal

What are birds of prey?

Birds of prey are the hunters, or the big predators, among the birds. They feed, or *prey*, upon other forms of animal life. In North America, some birds of prey are the hawks, falcons, kites, vultures, condors, ospreys, owls, and eagles.

A more exact word to use is *raptor*. Raptors are birds that use their extremely good eyesight and their strong, sharp claws—called *talons*—to capture prey. Sometimes raptors clasp their food in their talons and carry it to their nests. Raptors usually eat squirrels, rabbits, mice, shrews, birds, and other small animals.

Do fish drink water?

It depends on where they live. Freshwater fish don't drink; water soaks in through their gills and skin. They can't control how much water comes in, so they urinate often to get rid of extra water.

Saltwater fish have just the opposite problem—a lot of water soaks *out* of their bodies and into the salty ocean. They drink large amounts of water to keep from shriveling up. The salt that comes in with the water they drink goes out with their droppings or through special cells located in their gills. They almost never have to urinate.

Why do raccoons always wash their food?

The answer is that raccoons *don't* wash their food. Raccoons catch most of their food in shallow water. They feel around with their front paws for crayfish, tadpoles, and small fish. Many people who see this think they are washing the animals before they eat them.

A FISHY STORY ABOUT GIANT CLAMS

Have any of your friends told you about deep-sea divers who were killed by giant clams? Well, don't believe them. Scientists say the killer-clam stories just aren't true. Giant clams rest peacefully on coral reefs in the Indian and Pacific oceans with their yard-long shells open. Even if a pearl-hunting diver accidentally stepped into a giant clam, the diver would have plenty of time to escape— giant clams close their shells *very* slowly.

How do koala bears live if they don't drink water?

Koalas don't drink water because they get all the water they need by eating the leaves and shoots of eucalyptus trees. The leaves and shoots have enough moisture in them to satisfy the koala's need for water. Koalas live in the tree-tops and seldom come down.

Do grasshoppers really spit tobacco?

No. The brown fluid they "spit" is saliva, much like that in people's mouths. The saliva is made in glands that look like tiny bunches of grapes. It contains a chemical which helps the grasshopper digest the plant material that it eats. The saliva in people's mouths serves the same purpose.

How can a snake swallow a big mouse or a bird?

The bones of a snake's lower jaw are loosely connected to each other and to the bones of the upper jaw. A snake can separate these bones to swallow prey much larger than its normal mouth size.

What is North America's most poisonous snake?

The most poisonous snake in North America is the rattlesnake. Its cousins, the cottonmouth (also known as the water moccasin) and the copperhead, are also very dangerous—and they don't have rattles on their tails to give warning.

Glands on each side of a poisonous snake's head make and store venom. Venom is a sort of poisonous saliva. It helps the snake to kill and digest its prey. Tiny tubes carry the poison from the venom glands to two fangs, one on each side of the top jaw near the front. The fangs are hollow and pointed and longer than the other teeth. When the snake bites, the venom comes down through the fangs and into its victim.

Typical jaw structure

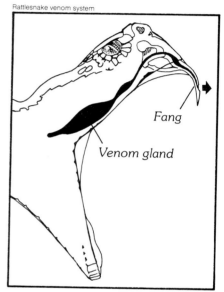

Rattlesnake venom system

Fang

Venom gland

KILLER INSECTS

Look at a field colorful with daisies, goldenrod, and Queen Anne's lace. Pretty, isn't it? Now look closer.

Bees, wasps, flies, beetles, and bugs come and go. Some munch the leaves. Others gather nectar or pollen. But many hope to eat their fellow visitors to the field.

In egg-laying season, wasps hunt spiders, flies, beetles, and other prey. The wasps sting and paralyze their victims. Then they carry the bodies off to the egg chambers in their nests to serve as food for the newly hatched wasp larvae.

The ambush bug is another scary hunter. It hides among the flowers. When an insect it wants to eat comes by, it reaches out and holds its victim down with its strong legs. Then it pokes its long, hollow snout into the insect and drains its body fluid as if it were sipping soda through a straw.

Even a bare path through the field may be filled with danger. Inside small, round holes, larvae of the tiger beetle—called *doodlebugs*—wait for their insect dinners to wander by. A doodlebug's curved jaws just reach the edge of the hole. Inside the hole, the doodlebug grips the walls with a hook near its tail so it can pull hard downward. When an unsuspecting insect steps near the jaws, the doodlebug grabs it, jerks it into its hole, and eats it.

That is the story all through the field—wasps kill beetles, spiders kill wasps, all to get food to live.

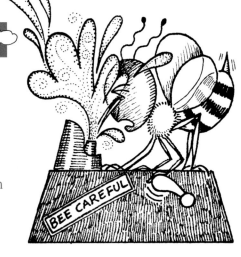

Do bees ever get thirsty?
Yes they do. Usually, nectar in flowers has enough water for bees. But often bees drink from puddles or dew on leaves. They may even visit decaying fruit to get a drink.

What do turtles eat?
Different kinds of turtles eat different kinds of food. Fresh-water turtles eat fish, frogs, snails, crayfish, carrion (dead animals), and plants. Sea turtles eat seaweed and small animals attached to the plants. Tortoises, or land turtles, eat all sorts of things, including mushrooms, grass, fruit, carrion, and insects.

Box turtles are fond of raspberries and strawberries. Sometimes they eat so much they can't fit all the way back into their shells. Now that's really eating yourself out of house and home!

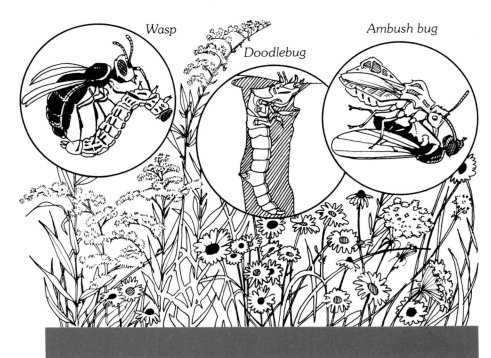

Wasp

Doodlebug

Ambush bug

SHARK TEETH, SHARP TEETH

The teeth of many sharks are triangular and have sawlike edges that are incredibly sharp. These teeth can easily cut all the way through a swordfish's tail or slice large chunks out of whales, which are much larger than sharks.

Though these sharks' teeth are as keen edged as razors, they probably never become dull. They don't have a chance to. The sharks lose their teeth and replace them with new ones so fast there is not much time for a tooth to lose its cutting edges. Some sharks get completely new sets of teeth about every two weeks. How? They have rows of teeth, one behind another. When a tooth gets torn out, a tooth from the next row back moves forward to replace it.

White shark

How long can seals hold their breath?

Weddell seals, which live in the Antarctic, can hold their breath over 40 minutes! While looking for food, one seal stayed under water a little longer than 43 minutes before surfacing to get air. Most human beings can hold their breath for only about one minute.

Seals have special "tricks" that let them go without breathing for so long. They slow their heartbeat down from 150 beats per minute to as few as 10. Also, they increase the supply of blood to their brain and vital organs, where it is needed most, and decrease the supply to other parts of their body. By doing these things they reduce the amount of oxygen they need.

Can animals get cavities?

Animals do get cavities, but far less often than humans do. Their teeth seem to fight the bacteria that cause decay. Maybe that's partly because many animals gulp their food without chewing it. Also, because of the way animal teeth are shaped, food doesn't stick between them long enough to cause problems. Animals also eat foods that are better for their teeth than some of the foods humans eat. Scientists have found that if rats eat a lot of sugar, they get cavities.

Can fish drown?

Under certain conditions, yes. Fish breathe oxygen, just as you do. They do this by making water go through their gills. The water contains oxygen that comes from the air or is given off by algae and other water plants. The gills take the oxygen out of the water. If the water doesn't have enough oxygen, the fish suffocate, which is what happens when any animal drowns.

Do animals have "baby" teeth?

Yes, they do! Normally an animal has two sets of teeth. The first set is complete except for molars—there are incisor teeth for cutting, canine (sharp, pointed) teeth for grabbing, and premolars for grinding food. These "baby" teeth fall out as the animals get older. They are replaced by permanent teeth, including molars.

Why do worms come above ground when it rains?

Because they will suffocate if they stay in their flooded burrows too long.

Earthworms have no lungs or gills; they breathe through their thin, moist skin. When they are in dry burrows, their skin takes in all the oxygen they need from the air found between loose bits of soil. When their burrows are flooded, earthworms take oxygen from the water. But after a while, they use up all the oxygen in the water and have to escape from their burrows or drown. That is also why you see so many dead earthworms in puddles.

Are tusks really teeth?

Yes. Tusks are extra-long curved teeth. Walruses, boars, and elephants have tusks. In elephants, tusks first appear when a youngster is about 30 months old. They keep on growing throughout the elephant's life. A bull (male) elephant's tusks even grow faster as he gets older! The heaviest pair of tusks ever found were from a bull. One tusk weighed 214 pounds, the other one 226 pounds; together, the tusks weighed 440 pounds.

The tusks of females are much smaller and lighter. The record weight is 56 pounds for one tusk.

Elephants use their tusks to defend themselves, to strip bark off trees, and to lift and shove things.

Do animals cry?

Many land animals produce a liquid that looks like tears and keeps their eyes moist and clean. But most animals do not cry the way you do.

When you are upset, muscles around your eyes tighten and squeeze your tear glands. Tears fall from your eyes.

Animals such as dogs don't have those muscles in their faces. Other than people, only great apes and a few kinds of monkeys sometimes shed tears when they are upset.

What does a spider see with all its eyes?

Most spiders have eight eyes. In some spiders those eyes work as a "team": one pair locates an insect, one pair judges distance, and one pair directs the spider's leap. That leaves a pair on top of the spider's head to see enemies which might be sneaking up from behind.

Jumping spider

This party is really a "bawl"!

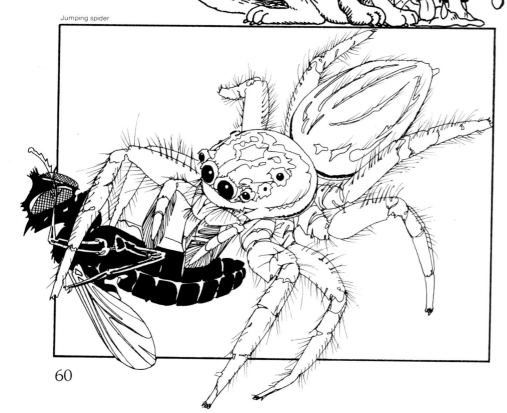

Can music charm snakes?

No. Snakes are deaf. What charms them is the swaying of the snake charmer's flute. Waving a stick slowly back and forth in front of a snake would work as well. (Don't you try it though! Snake charmers know just how close to get.)

Do a bird's eyes water when it flies fast?

No. Birds have a special eyelid in the corner of each eye close to the beak. These extra eyelids are called *nictitans* (NICK-tih-tans). Most often they are used to clean the eyes. When a bird blinks, the nictitans glide over the eyeballs. They remove grit and leave a soothing oil. But when a bird dives into water or flies fast, the nictitans serve as goggles. They cover the eyes and then stay in place. The nictitans are clear, so the bird can still see where it is going.

Do insects have ears?

Insects hear sounds, but they don't have ears like yours.

Flies, gnats, and mosquitoes have special hairs on their antennae that are sensitive to sound vibrations. Like you, grasshoppers, crickets, cicadas, and some butterflies and moths have tympanic (tim-PAN-ick) membranes (skin stretched tightly over openings). But these "eardrums" are located on the abdomens of cicadas and some grasshoppers and on the front legs of crickets! With their "ears" so far apart, these insects can easily tell what direction a noise is coming from.

How do fish hear?

With their ears! Fish have no outer ears or eardrums to catch sound vibrations, but they do have inner ears. They are located under the skin on each side of the head. Sound vibrations are carried to their inner ears through their bodies. Most fish cannot hear nearly as sharply as you do. But they can hear sounds that are made in water and loud sounds made above the water.

Where are birds' ears?

A bird's ears are on each side of its head. They are covered by feathers. Birds' ears have eardrums, middle ears, and inner ears, but no outer ears like you have.

"EAR" CONDITIONING

African elephants' ears sometimes measure as much as six feet long and five feet across! Those ears can really flap, too. They act as an air conditioner. Millions of tiny blood vessels bring warm blood from the elephant's body to the surface of the ears. By flapping its ears, a hot elephant can cool its blood and thus lower its body temperature. Sometimes elephants squirt water over their ears with their trunks. Then they flap their ears to create a breeze. The breeze evaporates the water and further cools the blood. That is a very handy trick when you have to stand in the blistering African sun!

Asian elephants have much smaller ears. They measure about two and a half feet long and one and a half feet wide.

How does a hammerhead shark use its hammer?

No one knows for sure. Some scientists think hammerheads use their heads for steering as they glide through the water. Other scientists think that having such wide heads helps the hammerheads search for food, since their eyes and smelling organs are on the ends of the hammer.

Why do beetles have two sets of wings?

The inner set of wings is used for flying. The hardened outer

Scarab beetle

wings are for protection. Because of them, a beetle can crawl in cracks or under bark without harming its abdomen or delicate flying wings. The hard wings may also keep a beetle from drying out and protect it from enemies.

Can insects live with their heads cut off?

Yes, but only for a short while. Insect bodies have three divisions: head, thorax, and abdomen. Amazingly enough, each division can live—for a brief time—even when it has been separated from the others. If the head is removed, the thorax and the abdomen can live until they starve. If the abdomen of a moth is removed, it can still be fertilized by a male and even lay eggs that will hatch. Heads that are removed can still bite.

Do deer antlers really fall off every year?

Indeed they do! Deer shed their antlers each winter after the mating season. Soon after that, two lumps appear on their heads. These lumps develop into full-grown antlers by the next fall.

During spring and summer, the new antlers are soft and tender and covered by a thin skin with fine hair called *velvet*. Blood in the velvet brings food to the antlers, which are made of bone. As the antlers reach full size in fall, the velvet dries up and the deer scrape their antlers against small trees to remove it.

Finally, in winter, the antlers themselves drop off, sometimes one at a time, sometimes both at the same time. Losing antlers doesn't hurt the deer a bit.

Only the male deer, or bucks, have antlers. They use them to fight for mates and for the right to lead the herd.

Velvet coming off antlers

TALES OF TAILS

Tails may seem strange to you, but they are useful pieces of equipment. A bird without a tail would have a hard time taking off and landing. A tailless fish would be like a submarine without an engine and rudder.

Jumping animals, such as squirrels, mice, and kangaroos, use their tails for balance and steering. The kangaroo's thick, strong tail also functions as a portable chair, forming a tripod with the hind legs when the animal sits down.

Many tree-dwelling animals have developed tails that are as useful as hands and feet for climbing and holding on. Such animals can hang onto limbs by the tail alone. That leaves their hands and feet free to gather food or groom themselves. The spider monkey's tail is so sensitive it can pick up bits of food as small as a peanut.

But perhaps a tail's most important job is to protect its owner's life. Many creatures' tails are defensive weapons or deceiving devices that may save the owners from being killed. Some lizards have lost parts of their tails while escaping enemies, but lived to grow new ones.

Do centipedes have 100 legs and millipedes 1,000 legs?
No. The bodies of centipedes and millipedes are divided into a number of segments on which their legs grow. Centipedes, whose name means "hundred-footers," have one pair of legs on each segment. Most centipedes have about 15 pairs of legs, or 30 legs; the longest have 173 pairs.

Millipedes, or "thousand-footers," have two pairs of legs on each segment. But they don't have a thousand legs. The most any millipede in the world has is 355 pairs.

Millipede

A COAT FOR ALL SEASONS

A snowshoe hare's coat is brown in summer and white in winter. The brown summer coat blends in with dry leaves and grass and helps the hare hide from its enemies. But as the days grow shorter, the hare begins to shed its brown coat and grow its white one. The feet, ears, and the front of the head turn white before the back does. It takes about 10 weeks for the new coat to grow in. By winter the hare matches the snow, except for its eyes and the black tips of its ears. Now it is ready for a new season of hiding from its enemies.

How many feathers does a bird have?

It depends on the bird. Big birds usually have more feathers than little birds. Somebody once counted the feathers on a Plymouth Rock hen and found 8,325. Another curious plucker counted 25,216 feathers on a whistling swan. Someone else patiently plucked 940 tiny feathers from a ruby-throated hummingbird.

Why do snakes have scales?

The scales that cover a snake's skin slow down the evaporation of water from its body.

Amphibians—frogs, salamanders, and toads—don't have scales. They lose water through their skin very quickly and must stay where it is moist. But snakes and other reptiles, protected by scales, are able to live in some of the driest places on earth.

Can a turtle crawl out of its shell?

No. A turtle's shell is a part of its body. Portions of the shell are made up of the turtle's flat ribs. The turtle's backbone is also firmly attached to the shell. If you ever find an empty shell, chances are the turtle died and the soft parts of its body either rotted away or were eaten by insects, birds, or other animals.

Do toads shed their skin?

Yes. So do frogs and all other amphibians.

When a toad grows, its skin doesn't grow with its body. Instead, the toad grows a new skin underneath the old one. Finally the old skin is too tight and needs to come off.

The toad starts to shed its old skin by puffing itself up with air, letting the air escape, then puffing itself up again. At last the old skin splits down the back. Then the toad wriggles until it pulls its front feet free. This skin comes off just like a glove.

Next the toad uses its front feet to pull the old skin from the rest of its body. As the toad sheds, it shoves the old skin right into its mouth—and eats it!

Why are some walruses pink?

Walruses, especially old males, don't have much hair on their skin to protect them from the sun. When they snooze on the beach in the hot sun, blood vessels located just below their skin swell up. The swollen vessels make the skin look pink. The hotter the walruses get, the pinker they become!

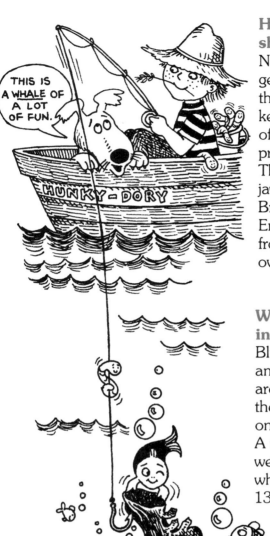

How big do great white sharks get?

No one is sure *how* big they get! Many scientists believe that great white sharks just keep on growing until they die of disease or injury. (They probably don't die of old age.) The biggest great white shark jaws ever found hang in the British Museum in London, England. The shark they came from is estimated to have been over 36 feet (10.8 m) long.

What is the biggest animal in the world?

Blue whales are the biggest animals in the world. They are so big they make elephants, the largest animals that live on land, look like dwarfs. A male African elephant may weigh up to 8 tons, but a blue whale could tip the scales at 135 tons—if a scale could be found large enough to hold its immense 100-foot-long body!

What is the oldest animal on earth?

The longest-lived animals of all are turtles. A very lucky bog turtle, just 3-1/2 inches (9 cm) long, could live 100 years. The record animal age is held by a Marion's tortoise from the Seychelles, islands in the Indian Ocean. It lived at least 152 years in captivity!

A mouse would be quite old if it lived 3 years. A chipmunk might live 8 years. Most whales live 20 to 30 years. Among mammals other than humans, elephants live the longest, often about 60 years.

A robin may warble for 8 years; thrushes may sing for 10. Ten years is old for a wild herring gull, but one pet gull lived for 44 years. The greatest life span for birds is held by the parrots, which can live to be 70.

How old do water animals get? An eel may live 19 years before it breeds and dies. Barnacles can live for almost 3 years.

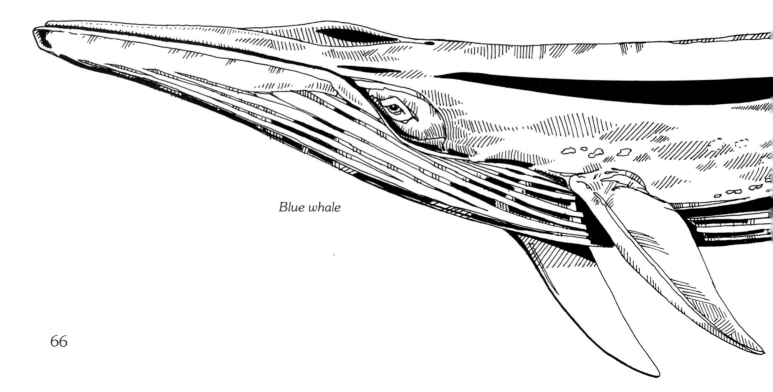

Blue whale

The story is different for the mayfly. This insect lives under water for up to 3 years. But as an adult it flits in the air for only one or two days and then dies. Cicadas may take 2 to 17 years to develop into winged adults, depending on the kind. As adults they are active for only a few weeks —just long enough to mate and start another brood.

So the length of life varies greatly among creatures. The important question in nature is not how long an animal lives, but how many of its offspring live on after it.

Does an elephant go to a special graveyard when it knows it is dying?
This is a well-known myth, but no one has ever found an elephant graveyard any place except in the movies. Elephants die anywhere, just as all other animals do.

Even though the elephant graveyard is a myth, there are some very interesting facts about how elephants treat their dead. Elephants become strongly attached to other elephants in their herds. They may watch over the body of a relative or "friend" after death. Sometimes elephants carry away the tusks or bones of a dead elephant. There are also reports of elephants burying bodies they find in their travels —even bodies of human beings! —with branches or soil.

What are the smallest and largest birds in the world?
The bee hummingbird of Cuba is the smallest bird in the world. It measures only two and one eighth inches from the tip of its bill to the tip of its tail. The largest bird is the ostrich of Africa. This flightless giant may reach a height of eight feet and weigh up to 345 pounds.

THE SMALLEST MAMMAL

The Mediterranean shrew is the tiniest mammal in the world. It is only 1-1/2 inches long. Looking much like a common gray mouse, the shrew is considered by some people to be the fiercest animal on earth. It fears nothing, and it will attack, kill, and eat enemies that are twice its size.

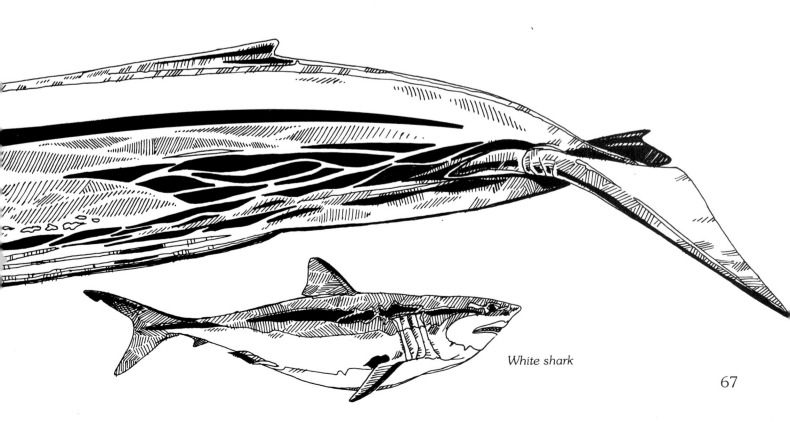

White shark

67

AN INVISIBLE MOTH

Do porcupines shoot their quills at their enemies?
No. The 30,000 or so quills—which are special hairs—are attached very loosely to the porcupine's skin. When a threatened porky smacks an enemy with its tail, the sharp quills stick in the *enemy's* skin as they pull loose from the *porky's* skin. The attacker is left with a face full of quills, and the porcupine usually escapes.

Porcupines grow new quills to replace the ones they lose.

Some animals can get the best of the porcupine. The worst enemy is the fisher, which looks like a weasel. A fisher can flip over a porcupine and rip open its soft belly, where there are no quills. Bobcats, wolves, and even great horned owls will sometimes tangle with porkies, often to their sorrow.

Can tarantulas kill people?
Tarantulas are poisonous, but not deadly to humans. People who have been bitten say it feels like a bee sting. Chances are a person will never be bitten by one of these beady-eyed creatures; they're quiet and secretive and attack only in self-defense. Some people even keep tarantulas as pets!

Would you believe this flower is really a moth? It is. It is a Mimallonid (My-MAL-o-nid) moth and lives in the jungles of Brazil. To make itself "invisible" by looking like a faded flower, the moth holds its wings up and folds its tail up, back, and over its head. It can stay in that position for hours.

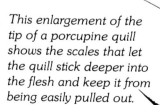

This enlargement of the tip of a porcupine quill shows the scales that let the quill stick deeper into the flesh and keep it from being easily pulled out.

Does an electric eel really make electricity?

Yes. An electric eel's body has layers of tissue, one under the other, exactly like the plates in a car battery. Chemicals in the eel's body flow from the head to the tail through these tissues and produce the electric current, the same as that in a battery.

Electric eels have been known to produce as much as 800 volts. That would stun or even kill a man or a horse. Even a little six-inch-long eel can send out about 300 volts. Eels use strong shocks when defending themselves and weaker shocks when stunning fish for their food.

The electric eel is not a true eel. It is a South American fish related to the carp and catfish.

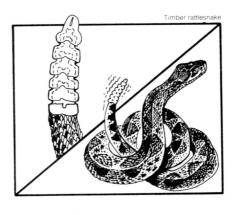
Timber rattlesnake

How does a rattlesnake's rattle make noise?

A rattlesnake's rattle is a modification of the scale that covers the tip of the tail. The rattle is built like a stack of tiny teacups. Each cup is attached to the next, and each has three small bumps on it. When the snake shakes its tail (about 50 times each second!), the bumps of one cup tap against the next cup. The tapping is so fast it sounds like a *hissss* rather than a rattle.

Rattlesnakes rattle for the same reason dogs growl. It's their way of saying *stay back!*

Why do some crabs have missing legs?

A crab will break off a leg if it needs to escape from an enemy that has a hold of it or if its leg gets stuck between two rocks. The leg breaks easily at the third joint, and it heals quickly. Each time the crab molts, or sheds, its shell, the stub of the missing leg will be a little longer. After several molts, the leg looks just like new!

Is the skin of toads poisonous?

Yes. Many of the lumps on their bumpy brown skin contain glands that ooze a milky poison. Most creatures that try to eat a toad wind up with a very sore mouth and throat.

If you catch a toad, wash your hands afterwards. The poison from the toad's skin usually will not harm your skin, but if it gets in your eyes it may irritate them.

Some toads urinate when they are grabbed, but the urine is not poisonous.

69

How do fish escape their enemies?

Many fish just speed and zig-zag to safety. Others blend with their surroundings to hide from enemies. Some even dig into the mud or sand and disappear from sight.

In Florida, young spadefish are the color and shape of the mangrove tree seed pods which lie on the sand beneath them. Young mangrove leaf fish wrinkle their long fins and sink slowly, looking like dead leaves. The featherlike fins of lionfish match branches of coral; and long, skinny pipefish (like the one in the photograph to the right) look like the waving seaweed among which they live. Stonefish, the most poisonous of all fish, look as lifeless as rocks on the ocean floor.

Some fish have other tricks. Catfish have sharp spines on their fins which they jab into their enemies. Porcupine fish swell themselves up to become large, spiny balls that look scary and are hard for most predators to swallow.

Are gorillas as fierce as they look?

No, they are almost the opposite—quite shy. When they beat their chests and roar, they are just trying to scare their enemies away by bluffing. A few gorillas have rushed at scientists who were studying them, but they have always stopped before reaching them. The scientists were not harmed. However, when gorillas are attacked, they use their sharp teeth to protect themselves.

How do lizards protect themselves?

When threatened, lizards will usually run away. If they can't, they have a trick or two for self-defense. They may try to scare off the attacker by puffing themselves up and hissing. Or, if an attacker grabs a tail, some lizards just break it off and escape. In time, the tail grows back.

Lizards also fight back by biting or lashing out with their tails. One, the horned toad (which is not a toad but a lizard), even squirts jets of blood from glands behind its eyes to scare off enemies.

Can a skunk aim its spray?

Yes. A skunk's aim is accurate up to 15 feet. A skunk warns its enemies by raising its black-and-white tail. If the enemy doesn't run away, the skunk whirls and shoots stinging, smelly liquid at the tormentor's face and eyes from a gland beneath its tail. There is enough liquid to shoot four or five shots in a row.

Do all animals fight?

Most animals will fight if they have to, but usually they try other ways of protecting themselves from enemies. Running away is one defense. Pronghorn antelope and giraffes and other fast four-footed animals do that. Hiding is another way. Baby deer (fawns) lie extremely still when a coyote or other predator approaches. The white spots on their brown coats blend in with the shadows and bright light around them. Other animals have even better camouflage. Certain moths have colors that make them look like the bark of the tree on which they land. It is very hard for birds to see them. Some animals, like badgers, use powerful leg muscles and big claws to dig holes in the ground very quickly. Then they hide in the holes. A few animals, like crabs and lizards, can even lose parts of their bodies and still live. However, many animals that are attacked will fight back by kicking, biting, ramming, or clawing their enemy.

IN SELF DEFENSE

Baby fulmars (FULL-mars), which live in the North Pacific and Arctic Oceans, spit to protect themselves. When gulls and eagles attack to eat the young birds, the chicks spit at them. They send out jets of bad smelling, partly digested food. They spit hard and they spit to hit, but their aim is not always very good.

Sometimes the chicks spit at their own family by mistake, so the parent fulmars cackle as they approach the nest. They land at a distance and keep cackling, as if telling the chicks, *Don't spit! It's your parents!*

Take that, you turkey!

Do animals talk?

Many animals do talk to each other, but not with words. Animals use sound, color, odor, and movement to communicate.

Animals can tell each other of possible danger. When a marmot first sees an approaching predator, it warns its neighbors with a whistle. A pronghorn antelope signals danger by raising its rump hairs. The hairs reflect light and make flashes so bright that other antelope up to four miles away can see them.

Ants use an odor language when gathering food. When an ant finds food, it goes back to the nest, depositing bits of scent along its trail. Other ants then pour out of the nest and follow the trail of smells to the food supply.

A bee tells others in the hive where it has found food by wobbling and twisting around in a pattern. Its movements tell the distance and the direction to the nectar.

Mockingbird

How do frogs make sounds with their mouths closed?

When a frog gets ready to croak or peep, it takes a big gulp of air that swells out its throat sac. To hold the air in, the frog closes its mouth and nostrils. Then it pumps the air back and forth between its lungs and mouth. As the air moves, it vibrates the vocal cords in the frog's throat. The puffed-out sac helps to make the sound much louder.

Do birds sing because they are happy?

Sometimes they do. At least some scientists think so. But most of the time birds sing for a very different reason.

Their singing is actually a warning to other birds to stay out of their territory. A territory is an area that an animal, usually the male, claims as its own. No other families of the same species are welcome. Birds are constantly screaming at outsiders, whether they can see them or not. This screaming is what we call a bird's song, and it is usually enough to keep an outsider away.

FOOD!

PICNIC

ow ow OWOOOOoooo

Many a cowboy in movies about the old West gets a creepy feeling at night when he hears the howl of a lonely wolf. But the popular belief that wolves howl at night because they are lonely is not true. Wolves howl to talk to each other, and there are many things to talk about.

Wolves live in packs that stake out large territories for hunting and rearing families. Often, members of a pack howl just to keep in touch with each other when they are hunting far apart.

A pack of wolves likes to keep other packs out of its territory. But fighting is hard, dangerous work—and wolves would rather spend their time hunting for food and resting. So, one wolf pack howls at another to warn it to stay out of its territory.

How do crickets sing?

Crickets don't have vocal cords, so they don't sing the way people do. They *fiddle* their songs, much as a violinist does. And not all crickets fiddle, either. Only the males make music. The male cricket lifts its wings. Then, using one wing as a violinist's "bow," he rubs that wing against the 130 or so tiny ridges on the other wing. This makes a clicking sound. The cricket rubs its wings together so quickly you can't hear the individual clicks.

Male crickets have several songs. One song is used to attract a mate. When a female cricket hears this special tune, she hops along the ground toward the sound and looks for the male. How does she hear him? With "eardrums" located on her knees! When she finds the male, he begins a new, different kind of song for her. Then they mate.

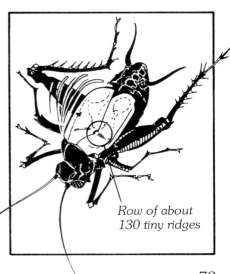

Row of about 130 tiny ridges

SOME ANIMALS CAN TALK WITH PEOPLE

O.K. Just one more.

smile

toothbrush

Dogs growl to scare people away. Cats "meow" for food. But all that's in animal language. Now some chimpanzees have learned to use the same sign language used by many humans who are deaf.

In the American Sign Language (ASL), the position of your fingers and the way you move your hands tell other people what you mean. You *show* ideas and words instead of saying them.

One captive chimp, Washoe, learned to say many words in sign language, including *listen, smile, more,* and *quiet.* She made up phrases —like "Sorry, sorry, hug me good" when she was naughty. She even warned herself "Quiet!" while running away from her teachers.

When Washoe was sent to live with other chimpanzees in a new home, she began using sign language to talk to them. They learned to use the language and seemed to understand each other.

The next step is a really big one. If Washoe has babies and teaches them the sign language, then a human language will have become an ape language, passed down from one generation to the next.

DOO WAH or DOO WAH

listen

What do fireflies use their lights for?

People turn on lights at night so they can see each other and where they are going. Fireflies use their lights to find other fireflies.

There are about 1,000 different kinds of fireflies, and each kind has its own special flash of light. That makes it possible for the males of a species to find females of the same species.

One kind of firefly in the eastern United States takes a "roller coaster" ride in the air while his light is on. He traces a "J" in the darkness with each blink.

Most of the fireflies seen flying at night are males. The females stay on the ground and flash back responses to the lights of the males. When the male sees the correct flash of light on the ground, he lands near it. Then the male and female mate.

Can fish make sounds?

They sure can. Drumfish got their name from the drumming sound they make during their mating season. These fish make the sound by quickly tightening and loosening certain muscles in their bodies.

If you ever frighten a grouper, it will probably make a loud *whomph* before its swims off. This sound is made when the fish closes its mouth and pushes water through its gills.

There's even a group of fish called *grunts*. These fish grind the teeth in their throat together to make strange scraping noises.

If you're under water and hear a noise that sounds like a boat whistle, don't be surprised. It might be the mating call of the toadfish. These strange-looking fish also make grunting noises.

Do spiders have vocal cords?

No, but some spiders can make sounds. Male wolf spiders, for instance, make noises that attract females. These spiders have sharp ridges on their feelers. During mating, a male rubs his feelers together, making a harsh scraping sound. It's hard to pick out the "melody," but the female really likes the serenade. And the noise warns other male wolf spiders to stay away.

Are bats as quiet as they seem to be?

No. Bats may be the noisiest creatures in the world! For many years no one knew just how noisy bats are, because most of their squeaks are too high-pitched for human ears to hear. Now scientists use special equipment to record bat squeaks and to play them back so human beings can hear them.

One eavesdropping scientist says that bat squeaks sound like the scream of a jet plane up close. Since there are millions and millions of bats around, perhaps it's just as well our ears can't hear all that screaming and shrieking!

Bats also make noises that humans *can* hear. These squeaks may be used to express such emotions as fear and to communicate with other bats.

Some bats even purr! When big brown bats are resting and contented, their bodies start to vibrate. This soft humming noise is called "body buzz." The buzzing stops when the bat falls asleep.

What is a school of fish?

Fish of the same kind and size sometimes live together in groups called *schools*. That helps them spot enemies. Many eyes are better than two! Also, fish can often locate more food if they swim together. Schooling fish find mates and escape enemies more easily. An enemy may attack a school of fish, get confused by so many flashing bodies, and not catch a single one.

Big schools can be really big! Sometimes millions and millions of herring swim together in a huge, crowded school that stretches for miles and miles under the sea.

Do animals have leaders?

Many social animals—elephants, wolves, monkeys, and others that live in groups—have leaders. Living together is not always easy. Even within a group, the animals compete for food, for mates, and for space. If fights were to get out of hand, the group might destroy itself. The leader keeps that from happening.

Sometimes the leader keeps order just by being there. One scientist discovered that rhesus monkey leaders might go for years without even snarling. But, if necessary, a quick whack with the back of a leader's hand would bring his group under control. Chimpanzee leaders also threaten and sometimes fight members of their group to keep order. Female elephants have been seen using their trunks to spank naughty young elephants!

Do bees ever live alone?

Yes. In fact, most kinds of wild bees live alone. In North America there are over 4,000 kinds of solitary bees.

Each female solitary bee builds her own nest and takes care of her own young. Among some kinds of solitary bees, females nest close together in the ground. Each female digs a tunnel with several side rooms. She stuffs each room with a ball of pollen and nectar. Then she lays a single egg, seals the room, and leaves. When the young bee hatches, it eats the food and leaves the tunnel. It may never see its mother.

Do all the ants in a colony work?

Yes, but they divide the chores. Whether in small colonies of a dozen ants or in large ones of over a million, there are three types of ants—and each type has its own job to do.

The *queen* ant spends her whole life laying eggs for the colony. This may be for as long as 15 to 20 years. She is totally waited on by the worker ants.

Most of the ants in the colony are *workers*. They are females that don't grow wings, usually are smaller than the queen, and can't have babies. Workers care for the queen and her offspring and fight off enemies. They also build, repair, and clean the nest. The workers' biggest job is to feed the colony.

At a special time of the year the *males* are formed. Their only job is to mate with new queens that are also formed at this special time. The males die after mating, and the new queens look for sheltered places to begin their own colonies.

PRAIRIE DOG TOWNS

In the early 1800's, pioneers heading west found mile after mile of prairie grassland dotted with mounds and undermined with tunnels. These were the homes of little grass-eating rodents. The pioneers called these barking animals "prairie dogs" and their underground homes "towns." One prairie dog town in Texas covered almost 25,000 square miles—about the size of West Virginia. It was said to have 400 million prairie dogs—almost twice the human population of the entire United States today. Smaller colonies were found in grasslands all the way up to Canada. Today, some can still be found in the Dakotas, Wyoming, and Texas.

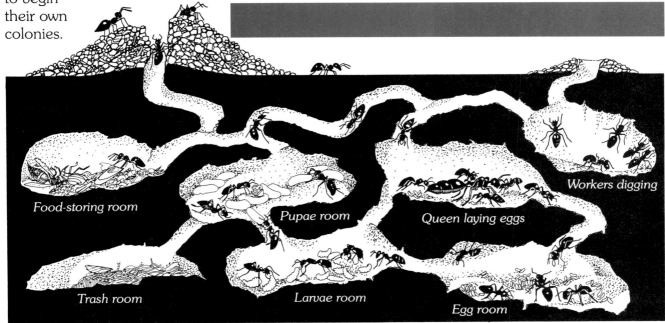

Food-storing room

Trash room

Pupae room

Larvae room

Queen laying eggs

Egg room

Workers digging

Do animals take baths?
Yes, animals bathe frequently. Most of you know that birds take baths in puddles and bird baths. They also bathe in dust and sand holes, and sometimes in the snow! But there are many other kinds of "baths" that animals take.

Kangaroo rats take dust baths by rolling in sand. As a rat rolls over and over, the sand acts as a brush and cleans its fur.

Even the earthworm takes a bath. At night, worms crawl out of their underground homes and bathe in the dew.

Elephants take dust baths and showers. To shower, they suck up water into their trunks and squirt it all over their bodies. If a baby elephant is near, it gets squirted too.

Many animal mothers give their babies tongue lickings to get them clean. That's what a mother tiger does. With her rough tongue she licks dirt off her furry cub.

Birds often comb, or *preen,* themselves with their bills. Some birds run their bills over their feathers to put ruffled ones in place. They also use their bills to spread oil from a gland near their tails. The oil waterproofs their feathers.

Why do crows put ants under their feathers?
Crows that do this are anting. Many other kinds of birds behave this way, but scientists aren't sure why.

Maybe the ants help the birds by eating lice and other pests that live among their feathers. Many ants' bodies contain a sharp-smelling liquid called *formic acid.* When a bird crushes an ant and puts it under its feathers, the formic acid may clean the feathers or kill small pests.

Do animals wash their ears?
Some do. Bats and rabbits are two creatures that take very good care of their ears.

Bats' ears must always be clean because bats find their way by listening to sounds (echo location). When washing, a bat puts the thumb of its winged front "hand" in its ear and twists it around and around to loosen the dirt. It cleans the rest of its furry body with its long, pink tongue.

A rabbit cleans its ears by pushing them forward with a foot so its tongue can reach them. Then it licks out any dirt that has collected in the long part of its ear.

Why do some insects rub their antennae with their front legs?
Rubbing their legs against their antennae is how insects keep their "feelers" clean. Bees have "combs" on their front legs with which they clean pollen off their sensitive antennae.

Ants have antennae-cleaning "brushes" on their "wrists." After cleaning their antennae, they lick the "brushes" clean. They also lick their bodies with their tongues.

Oxpecker on impala

Are there any doctors or dentists among animals?

Not exactly, but some kinds of animals help members of other species stay healthier by helping them keep clean.

The fierce moray eel needs help in ridding its mouth of sea lice. So it swims to a reef in the ocean where small fish called *wrasses* are darting about. The eel opens its huge mouth, which is full of needle-sharp teeth, and some of the wrasses swim into it and start cleaning. When they are finished, the eel swims away.

Certain kinds of birds—red-billed oxpeckers and egrets, for example—land on the backs of grass-eating mammals like impalas and cattle. The birds walk all over the mammals and peck ticks and flies off their skins. That helps the mammals stay healthy because fewer disease-carrying insects attack them. The birds are happy because they get an easy meal!

OUCH! DARN THOSE MOSQUITOES!!

Did you know that animals, even furry bears and foxes, get bitten by mosquitoes? They do, and they itch just as much as you do when you get bitten. What do you do? You scratch! —and so do animals. Animals have many different ways to scratch themselves. They use their tongues to lick itchy places, or a paw to reach behind an ear. Antlers make good scratchers for some animals.

Nibbling with teeth helps too. Some animals use the rough bark of trees for scratching. They rub against the trunk— back and forth, back and forth. Ooh, that feels good.

Not all scratching is to get rid of an itch. Many times it is a way for an animal to clean itself and spread oil on its feathers or fur. It also helps get rid of ticks and fleas and other pests.

Red fox

Drat! Missed again!

What are fins used for?

Mostly, fins are for swimming. The tail fin helps push fish forward when they swing their tails from side to side. The other fins help fish keep their balance or change direction. But some unusual fish use their fins for walking, flying, and even "fishing"!

The sea robin has leglike fins with which it walks along the ocean floor. The walking catfish of Asia uses its spiny fins, as well as its tail, to walk on land.

Flying fish use their side fins to glide as high as 20 feet above the water. Hatchet fish and butterfly fish really fly. They flap their fins as they skim above the water.

The frogfish has one fin that looks like a line and bait, which it dangles in front of its head. Smaller fish are lured right up to its waiting mouth and end up as a meal!

Do monkeys ever fall when they swing between trees?

Yes. It is not unusual to see a monkey favoring an arm or leg that it has broken in a fall.

Usually, though, monkeys don't fall because their bodies are specially adapted for swinging. Some kinds of monkeys are helped by having feet that curl and grip the branches. Some have rough finger pads that keep them from slipping. And some have tails that can hold onto tree limbs.

The champion trapeze artist is the gibbon. With its long, strong arms it can swing out and clear 45 feet between branches. In fact, gibbons are such skillful performers that, as they sail from branch to branch, they can snatch a bird right out of the air!

Flying fish

Walking catfish

Fantail goldfish

Frogfish

How does a snail move?

A snail moves by stretching and pulling muscles in its *foot*—the large, fleshy part of the snail's body that rests on the ground. A gland in front of the foot oozes a sticky slime to make it easier for the foot to slide along.

What keeps water striders from sinking?

A water strider's legs are covered with tiny, water-resistant hairs. These hairs keep the strider's legs from breaking through the surface of the water. Where the legs touch the water, the water sags into dimples that cast shadows on stream bottoms.

What insect looks like pepper and hops around in the snow?

The snow flea. This tiny critter has a slender tail that it curls under itself and hooks onto a catch under its body. When a snow flea releases the catch, the tail springs loose and catapults the snow flea into the air.

Why don't flies fall off ceilings and windows?

Flies have sticky pads on the ends of their legs. That's how flies can walk across ceilings or up smooth windowpanes. That sticky stuff also helps them carry disease germs from place to place. In addition, flies have tiny hooks on their feet. With these they "hook onto" any little roughness on a surface to make sure they won't fall off.

THE JET SET OF THE ANIMAL WORLD

Octopuses can crawl, swim, or *jet* around in the water. To use its jet, an octopus draws water into a cavity in its mantle (body) and then closes the opening. Next it contracts the muscles in the mantle and forces the water out through a tube called the funnel. The force of the water rushing out of the funnel propels the octopus. It is like blowing up a balloon and letting it go. The balloon shoots off in the opposite direction from the air spurting out the neck.

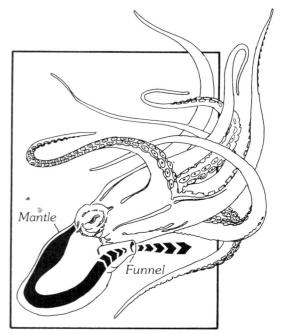

Mantle

Funnel

What are the fastest animals?

Everything in nature moves at its own pace, just the right speed to survive. If all the animals in the world were to race, the winner on land would be the cheetah (63 mph); the winner in the water, the sailfish (68 mph); and the winner in the air, the swift (106 mph). Falcons may reach nearly 200 miles per hour, but that's in a dive, not in level flight.

Dragonfly (18 mph)

Ostrich (30 mph)

Child, 10 years old (12 mph)

Pronghorn antelope (55 mph)

Pacific leatherback turtle (22 mph)

Dolphin (25 mph)

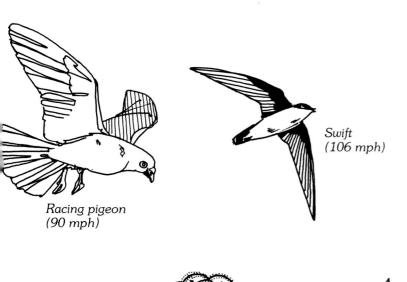

Racing pigeon
(90 mph)

Swift
(106 mph)

Peregrine falcon
(200 mph in a dive)

Cheetah
(63 mph)

Sailfish
(68 mph)

83

Are all migrations long?
No. Many animals only migrate short distances, some just a few miles. Elk, for example, spend the summer months grazing in the high mountain meadows of the West. When the first heavy snows fall, the elk herds begin to migrate down to the foothills and valleys. There they find protection from the fierce winter winds. Also, the snow is not as deep at the lower elevations. The elk can dig through the snow and eat the dried grass beneath. Bighorn sheep and muledeer also migrate up and down the mountains with the seasons.

Why do geese fly in a V formation?
It saves energy for the geese. When a goose flies, its wings churn up the air, leaving behind an air current. If another goose flies in this current, it can

get an extra amount of lift from its wings. When geese fly in a V formation, each bird is in just the right position to get a lift from the bird ahead. This makes less work for all the geese, except the leader. Often during migration, several geese in a formation take turns being the leader.

Geese aren't the only birds that migrate in a V. Some others are ducks, swans, gulls, ibises, and cormorants.

How fast do the wings of insects beat?

Flying insects are a lot like helicopters. Movement in their wings lifts them into the air and sends them scooting forward. Large insects may beat their wings at about 20 full up-and-down strokes a second. Flies and bees reach about 200 strokes a second; smaller bugs, 600 or more a second; and the tiny biting midge, an amazing 1,000 full strokes a second!

Desert locust (18 to 20 beats per second)

MAMMALS ON THE MOVE

Wildebeests, like the ones to the left, are among the few land mammals that make long migrations. During the dry season in central and southeastern Africa, groups of from 5 to 15 animals may travel 1,000 miles or more in search of food and water. Sometimes as many as 500,000 wildebeests come together at the few pastures on the Serengeti Plain that stay green during the dry season. Then the rainy season comes. The animals separate into small herds again and wander off, thriving on the great increase in the amount of food and water.

How do birds fly?

Birds' bodies are streamlined. Air slides smoothly past overlapping feathers; birds' noses and ears are just holes. In flight, birds pull their feet up under their feathers. Nothing sticks out to keep them from slicing smoothly through the air.

Birds' wings are specially shaped for the tough job of keeping birds airborne. The top surface of the wing arches upward and the bottom surface is nearly flat. As the air rushes past the wing, it pushes up against the flat bottom with a force called *lift*.

When a bird flaps its wings, it moves them in a figure 8— forward and down, then backward and up. The inner half of the wing, the arm, produces lift *upward* for support. The outer half, the hand, produces lift *forward* for movement, like an airplane's propeller.

COME ON IN! THE WATER'S FINE!

How can polar bears, seals, and sea otters stand cold water?

Polar bears and sea otters (but not seals) and many other mammals that live in water are protected by their thick fur. The fur has lots of hairs close together. When the animals swim, air bubbles get caught between the hairs. These bubbles help keep the water from reaching the animals' skins.

Seals and polar bears (but not sea otters) have a thick layer of insulating fat beneath their skin. The fat keeps their body heat from being lost to the cold water.

COLD, BUT NOT COLD

Down

How do frogs breathe when they hibernate under water?

When frogs hibernate, the organs in their bodies work very slowly. The frogs need only a little oxygen to stay alive. There is some oxygen in the water around them, and the frogs take in enough through their skins.

Does cold weather hurt bumblebees?

Yes. In the fall of the year, all the bumblebees in a colony die. But, before dying, the colony produces up to one hundred new queens and males to hibernate through the winter months. Though most of these may also die, at least one of the queens usually survives the cold weather. In the spring, she lays her eggs and starts a new colony.

What happens to snakes in the winter?

In the late fall, snakes crawl into sheltered places such as caves, burrows, or pits. There they hibernate. Their bodies become cold and their breathing and heartbeat slow way down.

Sometimes large groups of snakes hibernate in the same place. In parts of the Canadian provinces of Manitoba and Saskatchewan, more snakes gather together in one place than anywhere else in the world. Ten or fifteen thousand garter snakes travel as far as ten miles so they can spend the winter tangled together in a single pit! When there are so many huddled together, they keep each other warm enough to survive the freezing weather.

Snakes usually awaken and begin to emerge from their winter homes during the warm days of May or June when the sun has melted the snow.

The *weather* may turn cold, but *birds* don't usually get cold. Their bodies stay between 101° and 112°F (depending on the kind of bird), partly because of their warm coat of down and feathers. Their downy inner plumage insulates them just as it insulates you when you sleep in a down-filled sleeping bag. A bird's outer feathers form a tight shell that keeps the wind out and the warmth in. On *really* cold days, the birds fluff up their feathers. That's like changing from a light-weight sleeping bag to a heavy one made especially for winter. Also, the birds shiver to keep their blood circulation high and squat down to cover their legs with their breast feathers.

Do bears hibernate?

No. Bears do spend most of the winter sleeping, but they're not really hibernating.

When an animal such as a woodchuck hibernates, his heartbeat and breathing slow down so much he looks as if he were dead. Also, his temperature drops; when you touch him, he feels cold. It's almost impossible to wake him up.

But bears are different.

During the fall, bears—like woodchucks—eat seeds and nuts until they have built up a layer of fat. They also find a warm den, crawl in, and doze off. But a bear's body stays warm. Its breathing slows down a bit, but not nearly as much as a hibernating animal's. If something disturbs a bear, it can wake up in just a few minutes. And sometimes, if the weather is mild, bears get up and stroll around in the snow.

GRIN & BEAR IT

BEAR-Y FRUIT FARM

RASP-BEARIES | STRAW-BEARIES | BLUE-BEARIES | BLACK-BEARIES | HONEY

Grizzly bear

WHAT'S MY NAME?

MY NAME STARTS WITH D.

What is the difference between . . .

Flying Ants and Termites?

Termites are usually pale and have soft bodies. Flying ants have hard bodies and are darker than termites.

Termites have straight antennae (feelers). Ant antennae have a crook in them.

Both flying ants and termites have two pairs of wings. In termites, the two pairs are about the same size. In flying ants, the back pair of wings is smaller than the front pair.

Like all insects, ants and termites have bodies that are divided into three parts —the head, thorax, and abdomen. Ants are pinched in where the thorax and abdomen join, giving them a thin "waist." In termites, the thorax and the abdomen are joined smoothly and there isn't a "waist."

Ant

Termite

Alligators and Crocodiles?

The crocodile has a tapering, narrow snout. The alligator has a broad, almost square snout. Two teeth in the croc's lower jaw can be seen outside of the upper lip when the croc's mouth is closed. When a gator's mouth is closed, all its bottom teeth are hidden.

Dolphins and Porpoises?

Dolphins are larger than porpoises and may have snouts that stick out almost like beaks. Porpoises are less than six feet (1.8 m) long and have rounder heads. Biologists tell them apart by the shape of their fins and teeth. When you go to a marine show, the animal you see leaping through hoops is probably a bottlenosed dolphin.

Dolphins and porpoises are not fish. They are mammals. That means that they are warm-blooded and that they nurse their young with milk.

Crocodile

Alligator

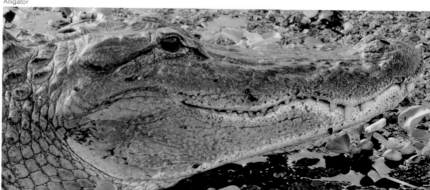

88

LONGER BY A HARE!

Hare

Rabbit

Rabbits and Hares?

Rabbits are smaller than hares and usually have shorter legs and ears. Newborn rabbits are blind and naked. Hares are born with their eyes open and are ready to scamper from danger just minutes after birth. Baby hares are also covered with short fur, so it's easy to remember this difference— baby hares have hair.

Turtles and Tortoises?

In the United States, people usually use the word *turtle* when they refer to the animals that live in the water. Both freshwater and ocean creatures are called turtles. The word *tortoise* is used for the animals that live on the land, such as the Galapagos tortoises, Texas tortoises, and gopher tortoises. An exception to this rule is the box turtle. The box turtle lives on land its whole life, but it isn't called a tortoise.

THINGS AREN'T ALWAYS WHAT THEY SEEM

Moth

Butterfly

That's a bumblebee to the left, and that's a moth above, right? Wrong. The "bee" is a moth, and the "moth" is a butterfly! You can tell that the "bee" is a moth because it has a thick, hairy body and holds its wings out flat when resting. The "moth" is identified as a butterfly by its slender antennae with bulbs at the tips and the way it holds its wings above its back while resting.

Turtle

Tortoise

89

NO LAUGHING MATTER

Laughing hyenas, also called spotted hyenas, really do laugh, but not the way you do when you hear a joke. Their "laughter" is a howl that only *sounds* like crazy human laughter. They howl loudest during the breeding season and when they are excited over something.

Why were passenger pigeons called *passenger* pigeons?
An old-fashioned meaning for the word *passenger* is a *traveler* or *migrant.* Two hundred years ago, these pigeons lived in enormous flocks of millions of birds that flew across the country. Because these birds migrated through an area, they were called *passenger* pigeons.

How did the black widow spider get its name?
This poisonous spider got its name from its color and from the female's reported habit of killing the male after mating.

Black widows really are black, except for the red hourglass marking on the underside of most black widows found in the United States. But the female does not always kill her mate. She does that only when she is unusually hungry.

A female black widow's poison is stronger than a rattlesnake's, but black widows seldom bite people. They prefer to hide in their webs in dark places.

Is the bald eagle bald?
No. Adult bald eagles have handsome heads of snowy white feathers. If you look in a dictionary, you'll see that one of the meanings of *bald* is "to have white feathers or fur on the head." So, the name *bald eagle* was given to this particular eagle to describe its appearance.

What is happening in the picture to the right?
These mallard ducks are grubbing for food at the bottom of the pond and letting you know that this is THE END!

90

Here's where to find out about...

Illustrations are in **boldface** type.

A

Aardvark: 52
Age: 66-67
Alligator: 45, 88, **88**
Ambush bug: 57, **57**
Ant: 26, 72, 77, **77,** 88, **88**
Ape: 53, 60, 70
Atmosphere: 16, **16,** 17

B

Banana plant: 31, **31**
Bat: 75, 78
Bean, Mexican jumping: 27, **27**
Bear: 79, 87, **87**
Bee: 21, 57, 72, 76, 78, 85, 86, 89
Beetle: 57, **57,** 62, **62**
Bighorn sheep: 84
Birds: 50, 54, **54,** 55, 60, 61, 63, 65, 67, 72, **72,** 78, 84-85, **84-85,** 86, **86**
   (see also individual listings)
Black widow spider: 90
Breathing: 59
Bristlecone pine: 32, **32**
Butterfly: 37, **37, 48,** 48-49, 89, **89**
Butterfly bush: 37, **37**

C

Cactus: 26, **26,** 40, **40**
Cardinal: 54, **54**
Caterpillar: 27, **27, 48,** 48-49
Catfish: 69, 70, 80, **80**
Centipede: 63
Cheetah: 50, **50,** 82, **82-83**
Chimpanzee: 74, **74,** 76
Chlorophyll: 30-31
Cicada: 61, 67
Clam: 55
Cocklebur: 26
Cockroach: 45
Coco de Mer: 27
Communication: 72-75
Condensation: 19, 20
Condor: 55
Conifer tree: 32, **32**
Continents, movement of: 8, 9
Copperhead: 56
Coral: 13, **13,** 15, 55
Cottonmouth: 56
Crab: 69, 71
Cricket: 61, 73, **73**
Crocodile: 47, **47,** 88, **88**
Crow: 78
Crystal: 12
Cypress: 35, **35**

D

Dandelion: 26, 31
Deciduous tree: 32, **32**
Deer: 21, 37, 62, **62,** 71, 84
Defense: 68-71
Devils Tower: 14, **14**
Dew: 19, **19**
Diatom: 40, **40**
Dinosaur: 44-45, **45**
Dog (wild): 51, **51,** 60, 74
Dolphin: **82,** 88
Doodlebug: 57, **57**
Dragonfly: 19, **19, 82**
Drumfish: 75
Duck: 51, 54, 85, 90, **91**

E

Eagle: 54, **54,** 55, 71, 90
Ears: 61, **61**
Earthquake: 10, 11
Earthworm: 54, 59, 78
Eel: 66, 69, 79
Egret: 79
Elephant: 49, 59, 61, **61,** 66, 67, 76, 78
Elk: 37, **37,** 84
Evaporation: 19, 20
Evergreen tree: 31, 32, **33**
Eyes: 60

F

Falcon: 55, 82, **83**
Fantail goldfish: **80**
Feather: 65, 86
Fighting: 70-71, 73
Fin: 80, **80**
Finch: 54
Firefly: 75, **75**
Fish: 34, 55, 57, 59, 61, 76, **76,** 79
   (see also individual listings)
Fisher: 33, 68
Flamingo: 54, **54**
Flower: 36, **36**
   (see also individual listings)
Fly: 57, 61, 79, 81, 85
Flying fish: 80, **80**
Food: 54-57
Fossil: 15, **44,** 44-45
Fox: 79, **79**
Frog: 18, 21, 57, 65, 72, 86
Frogfish: 80, **80**
Fulmar: 71
Fur: 64, **64, 65,** 79, 86

G

Geyser: 9, **9**
Giraffe: 37, 71
Glacier: 22, **22**
Goose: 6, **6,** 51, 84-85
Gorilla: 53, 70
Grass: 36, **36**
Grasshopper: 31, 56, 61
Grooming: 78-79
Grouper: 75
Grunt: 75
Gull: 66, 71, 85

H

Hailstone: 21, **21**
Hare: 64, **64, 65,** 89, **89**
Hatchet fish: 80
Hawk: 55
Herring: 76
Hibernation: 86-87
Home: 33, 52-53
Horned toad: 71
Hornet: 53
Hummingbird: 33, 46, 65, 67
Hurricane: 17, **17**
Hyena: 90, **90**

I

Iceberg: 22, **22**
Impala: 79, **79**
Insects: 21, 50, 61, 62, 65, 78, 79, 85
   (see also individual listings)
Ivy, poison: 39, **39**

J

Jumping spider: **60**
Jungle fowl of Australia: 52, **52**

K

Kangaroo: 63
Kelp: 40
Kite: 55
Kiwi: 46
Koala: 55

L

Leaf: **30,** 30-31, **31**
Lightning: 17
Lion: 31, 51, **51**
Lizard: 63, 71, **71**
Lobster: 45, **45**
Locomotion: 80-85
Log, nurse: 34-35, **35**
Lotus: 26

M

Mallow, marsh: 29
Mammoth: 44
Mangrove leaf fish: 70
Maple: 32
Marmot: 72
Mayfly: 66-67
Mermaid's purse: 46-47
Migration: 84-85
Millipede: 63, **63**
Minerals: 12
Mist: 20, **20**
Mockingbird: **72**
Mole: 11, 29
Monkey: 60, 63, 76, 80
Moon: 19
Moth: 27, **27,** 48-49, 68, **68,** 71, 89, **89**
Mountain: 12
Mouse: 11, 21, 29, 55, 63, 66
Muskrat: 29

N

Needle, pine: 31
Nest: 47, 52, **52,** 53
Nettle, stinging: 39
Nuthatch: 54, **54**

O

Oceans: 19, 20
Octopus: 81, **81**
Opossum: 33
Osprey: 55
Ostrich: 46, 67, **82**
Otter, sea: 40, **41,** 86
Owl: 54, 55, 68
Oxpecker: 79, **79**

P

Palm tree: 27, 32, **32**
Parents: 40, 47, **47, 50,** 50-51, **51**
Penguin: 54
Petrified wood: 15, **15**
Photosynthesis: 30
Pigeon: **83,** 90
Pipefish: 70, **70**
Planarian: 49, **49**
Polar bear: 22, **23,** 86
Pollen: 36, **36,** 39
Porcupine: 68, **68**
Porcupine fish: 70
Porpoise: 88
Prairie dog: 77, **77**
Pronghorn antelope: **36,** 71, 72, **82**
Pumice: 12
Pupa: 27, **48,** 48-49, **77**

Q

Quicksand: 15

R

Rabbit: 29, 33, 49, 55, 78, 89, **89**
Raccoon: 33, 55, **55**
Rain: 18, **18,** 19, **19**
Rainbow: 20, **20**
Raptor: 55
Rat: 11, 53, 59, 78
Rattlesnake: 56, **56,** 69, **69**
Redwood: 32
Reproduction: 46-49
Reptile: 50, 65
Robin: 54, 66
Rock: 12, 14, **14,** 15, **15**
Root: 28-29, **28-29,** 33, 35, **35**

S

Sailfish: 82, **82-83**
Salamander: 65
Sand: 14, **14,** 15
Sand dune: 14, **14**
Scorpion: 50
Sea horse: 47, **47**
Seal: 59, 86
Sea robin (fish): 80
Seaweed: 13, 40, **41,** 57
Seed: **26,** 26-27, **27**
Sequoia: 32, **33**
Shark: 46-47, 58, **58,** 62, 66, **67**
Shrew: 55, 67
Size: 66-67
Skin: 65
Skunk: 33, 71
Sky: 16, **16,** 17
Snail: 57, 81
Snake: 11, 56, **56,** 60, 65, 86
  (see also individual listings)

Snow: 22
Snow flea: 81
Spadefish: 70
Speed: 82, **82-83**
Spider: 50, 53, **53,** 57, 60, **60,** 75
  (see also individual listings)
Squirrel: 33, 55, 63
Steam fog: 20, **20**
Stomach: 37, **37**
Stonefish: 70
Sundew: 38-39, **39**
Sunfish, ocean: 49
Swallow: 21, 33
Swan: 54, 65, 84-85
Sweetroot: 29
Swift: 82, **83**

T

Tail: 63
Tarantula: 68
Teeth: 44, **44, 58,** 58-59
Termite: 52-53, 88, **88**
Territory: 72, 73
Thrush: 66-67
Thunder: 17
Tiger: 78
Toad: 65, 69, **69**
Toadfish: 75
Tornado: 18, 21, **21**
Tortoise: 66-67, 89, **89**
Touch-me-not: 26, **26**
Tree: 32-35
Turtle: 21, 34, 57, 65, 66, **82,** 89, **89**
Tusk: 59

V

Venus's flytrap: **38,** 38-39
Volcano: 6, **7,** 8, **8,** 11, 12
Vulture: 55

W

Walrus: 59, 65
Wasp: 53, 57, **57**
Water: 18-21
Waterspout: 21, **21**
Water strider: 81
Wave: 11, 20
Whale: 40, 49, 66, **66-67**
Wildebeest: **84-85,** 85
Wind: 16, **16,** 17, 20, 21
Wolf: 51, 68, 73, **73,** 76
Wolf spider: 75
Woodchuck: 33, 87
Woodcock: 54, **54**
Wrasse: 79

Y

Yellowstone National Park: 9

CREDIT WHERE CREDIT IS DUE.

Illustrations

All realistic and diagrammatic art is by Frank Fretz. All section dividers and cartoons, except as noted below, are by Roz Schanzer.

Page 6: (top) L. Kronquist/Photo Researchers; (bottom) © 1974 Roger Tory Peterson. **7:** Tui De Roy Moore. **8:** (bottom right) Jean Pidgeon. **9:** (top) M. P. L. Fogden/Bruce Coleman, Inc.; (bottom) Photographic Library of Australia. **10:** (top) SIPA Press/Black Star; (bottom center) George Hall/Woodfin Camp, Inc. **11:** Jean Pidgeon. **12:** (right) Jean Pidgeon. **13:** (all) Keith Gillett. **14:** (center) Gene C. Frazier. **15:** (left) Jean Pidgeon; (right) Joseph Muench. **16:** (top) Jean Pidgeon. **17:** (left) Jean Pidgeon; (right) Flip Schulke/Black Star. **18:** (art) Jean Pidgeon; (photograph) Steven C. Wilson. **19:** (right) John Shaw. **20:** (top) Peter G. Sanchez. **21:** (top right) Jean Pidgeon; (bottom) Dr. Richard Chesher/Photo Researchers. **23:** Frank R. Sladek/Tom Stack & Assoc. **26:** (bottom margin) Jean Pidgeon; (right) Eric Weiss. **27:** (top) Jean Pidgeon; (bottom left, center, and right) Ross E. Hutchins; (bottom margin) Jean Pidgeon. **30:** (top) Dick Smith; (center) John Shaw. **32:** (bottom) Marv Poulson. **33:** (left) Gene Ahrens/Bruce Coleman, Inc. **35:** (top) Ruth Kirk. **36:** (center) C. Allan Morgan. **38:** (top left) Runk/Schoenberger/Grant Heilman; (bottom center) Dr. William M. Harlow; (right) Robert W. Mitchell. **39:** (top) Andrew Skolnick; (center) Robert W. Mitchell/Tom Stack & Assoc.; (bottom) Preston. **40:** (bottom) Donna J. Wiker. **41:** Stephen J. Krasemann/DRK Photo. **45:** (bottom) Douglas Faulkner. **46:** (left, all) Dr. E. R. Degginger. **47:** (bottom) Jonathan Blair/Woodfin Camp, Inc. **48:** (top left) Jack Drafahl, Jr.; (top right, bottom left and right) Rachel Lamoreux; (center left and right) Dr. E. R. Degginger. **50:** George B. Schaller. **52:** (top center) Mary Lane Anderson/Photo Researchers. **53:** (top) Perry Shankle, Jr. **54:** (left) Stephen J. Krasemann/DRK Photo. **55:** (center) Wolfgang Obst. **56:** (bottom) Anthony Mercieca. **58:** Valerie Taylor/Ardea Photographics. **61:** Dr. M. P. Kahl. **62:** (top) Dr. Edward S. Ross. **63:** (bottom) J. A. L. Cooke/Oxford Scientific Films, Ltd. **64:** Paul E. Meyers. **65:** (top) Stephen J. Krasemann/DRK Photo; (bottom) Charlie Ott/Photo Researchers. **68:** (top) Kjell B. Sandved; (bottom) Jim Anderson. **69:** (center right) John L. Tveten. **70:** Jane Burton/Bruce Coleman, Inc. **72:** (top) Laura Riley/Bruce Coleman, Inc. **73:** (top) Tom McHugh/Photo Researchers. **74:** (all photographs) © Field Enterprises Educational Corporation. **75:** (top) Satoshi Kuribayashi/Orion Press. **76:** (top right) Douglas Faulkner. **77:** (center) Leonard Lee Rue III. **79:** (bottom) Leonard Lee Rue III. **80:** (center left) Dr. W. Stephens/Tom Stack & Assoc.; (center) Anthony Mercieca; (right) Jane Burton/Bruce Coleman, Inc.; (bottom left) Robert J. Shallenberger. **81:** (bottom) Jane Burton/Bruce Coleman, Inc. **84-85:** (bottom) Tom Nebbia. **85:** (top right) Stephen Dalton/NHPA. **87:** (bottom) Stephen J. Krasemann/DRK Photo. **88:** (center right and bottom right) Robert E. Pelham. **89:** (hare) Willis Peterson; (rabbit) Karl Maslowski; (moth) Dr. Edward S. Ross; (butterfly) Larry West; (turtle) Robert L. Dunne. **90:** (center) Peter Davey/Bruce Coleman, Inc. **91:** Stephen J. Krasemann/DRK Photo.

Text

The text is adapted primarily from Wise Old Owl's columns in *Ranger Rick's Nature Magazine.* A few entries are adapted from articles in *National Wildlife* and *International Wildlife* magazines and in other publications. (Unless otherwise stated, all entries are from *Ranger Rick's Nature Magazine.*)

Page 6: "Volcano in a Cornfield," by James R. Newton, October 1979; "Surtsey, Nature's Newest Child," by Lloyd E. Jones, Jr., May 1969; "The Goose That Lives in a Volcano," by Emily W. Hallin, July 1979.

Pages 8-9: "Our Wandering Continents," by Lloyd E. Jones, Jr., February 1974.

Page 11: "Earthquakes: Do Animals Know They're Coming?" by James R. Newton, May 1979.

Pages 12-13: "What Are Rocks Made Of?" by Barrie G. Klaits, May 1978, excerpted by permission of Macmillan Publishing Co., Inc., from *When You Find a Rock, A Field Guide* by Barrie G. Klaits, copyright © 1976 by Barrie G. Klaits; "The Great Barrier Reef," by Keith Gillett, November 1972.

Pages 14-15: "Devils Tower: Our First National Monument," by Gene C. Frazier, April 1971; "Sand Dunes Can Be Troublemakers," by Fay Venable, August/September 1979; "Is Sand Really Ground-Up Rocks?" adapted from *Come With Me to the Edge of the Sea* by William M. Stephens, copyright © 1972 by William M. Stephens, reprinted by permission of Julian Messner, a Simon & Schuster division of Gulf & Western Corporation; "Quicksand: Don't Let It Trap You," by Fay Venable, August/September 1972.

Pages 16-17: "Blue Skies and Rainbows," by Eleanor C. J. Horwitz, August/September 1971; "What Do You Know About the Wind?" by Sara B. Murphey, March 1967; "What is a Hurricane?" by Julia Fellows, August 1977; "Thunder," by Russell O. Wheeler, July 1975.

Pages 18-19: "What Do You Know About Rain?" by Sara B. Murphey, April 1967; "Weather, Whether or Not," by Sara B. Murphey, January 1971; "Weather or Not," by Beverly Mowbray, February 1976.

Pages 20-21: "Hail," by Thomas K. Keenan, August 1976; "What Makes Rainbows?" by Mark C. Blazek, July 1977; "Waterspouts!" by Michael J. Mooney, July 1978; "Weather, Whether or Not," by Sara B. Murphey, January 1971; "Weather or Not," by Beverly Mowbray, February 1976.

Page 22: "What Do You Know About Glaciers?" by Sara B. Murphey, March 1969; "Ice on the Move," by Ann Hudson Downs, August/ September 1975; "Courageous Ice Bear," by Ernie Holyer, December 1968.

Pages 26-27: "Saguaro, King of the Cactus," by Barbara J. Bigham, *National Wildlife,* February/March 1980; "Traveling Seeds," by Cheryl Morgan, November 1975; "The Mysterious Jumping Bean," by Ross E. Hutchins, January 1971.

Pages 28-29: "Plant Anchors," by Virginia Leaper, March 1978.

Pages 30-31: "Autumn Is a Painter," by Anthony J. Shanley, October 1967; "Wacky Fruit," by Tony Fusco, August/September 1976; "Tooth of the Lion," by Fred Johnson, May/June 1973; "13 Questions To Stump Your Friends," by Jerome M. Cowle, January 1973.

Pages 32-33: "12 Trees That Helped Build America," by Margo Duryeá, January 1968; "13 Questions To Stump Your Friends," by Jerome M. Cowle, January 1973; "Ranger Rick's Records," by Robert Gray, February 1975; "Tree-Top High Rise," by Barbara J. Porterfield, October 1971.

Pages 34-35: "Nurse Log," by Ruth Kirk, May/June 1972; "Trees with Knees," by Fay Venable, July 1972; "13 Questions To Stump Your Friends," by Jerome M. Cowle, January 1973.

Pages 36-37: "The Wonder of Grass," by Eleanor B. Heady, March 1971; "Backyard Bother," by Rudolf Freund, August/September 1976; "Plant a Butterfly Garden," by Bebe Miles, May 1968; "The Amazing 4-Chambered Stomach," by Jean Brody, July 1975.

Pages 38-39: "Plants That Eat Insects," by Avis Demmitt, November 1970; "Backyard Bother," by Rudolf Freund, August/September 1976.

Pages 46-47: "The Inside Story of the Egg," by E. A. Schano, May/ June 1971, adapted with permission of Edward A. Schano, Professor, Poultry & Avian Sciences, Cornell University; "Sharks," by James R. Newton, January 1977; "Pa Pa Parents," by Fred Johnson, December 1975.

Page 49: "Let's Split," by E. Norbert Smith, October 1975.

Pages 50-51: "Animal Mothers," by John Frederic, May/June 1970; "Run Red Wolf," by Alice Putnam, January 1977; "Two African Predators," by George Schaller, July 1972.

Page 57: "The Micro-Murderers," by Ned Smith, *National Wildlife,* August/September 1971.

Page 60: "Who's Looking at You?" by Sean Edmund, April 1969; "Eyes," by Constance P. Warner, February 1973.

Page 63: "Ends and Means," by Anker Odum, *International Wildlife,* May/June 1971.

Page 68: "Frog—Toad," by Fred Johnson, May/June 1974.

Pages 70-71: "Finny Friends," by Mariette Nowak, March 1978; "Mini-Dragons," by Fred Johnson, December 1973; "The Spitters," by Anita Gustafson, January 1980.

Pages 72-73: "Why Birds Sing," by George Lippert, March 1971; "Cree—Cree, Zeet—Zeet," by Patricia W. Spencer, March 1977.

Pages 74-75: " 'Hurry, Please,' Said the Chimpanzees," by Aline Amon, September 1977, adapted by permission of Curtis Brown, Ltd., copyright © 1975 by Aline Amon; "Fireflies," by Alan Linn, July 1969.

Pages 76-77: "Finny Friends," by Mariette Nowak, March 1978; "Do Fish Go to School?" by Beverly Mowbray, April 1975; "Ants," by Stephen J. Krasemann, April 1974; "Life in a Prairie Dog Town," by Ned Smith, *National Wildlife,* April/ May 1979.

Pages 78-79: "What Do You Do If You Don't Have a Bathtub?" by Ruth Jaeger Buntain, March 1972; "Itchers and Scratchers," by Lee Stowell Cullen, May 1979.

Page 80: "How They Swing Through the Trees," by Anker Odum, *International Wildlife,* November/December 1979; "Finny Friends," by Mariette Nowak, March 1978; "Skater Without Ice," by Jan Garton, August/September 1976; "Tales of Tails," by Natalie S. Rifkin, May/June 1975; "Hold On!" by Fred Johnson, August/September 1972; "The Octopus," by Russ Kinne, October 1968, adapted with permission from Russ Kinne.

Page 82: "Who's the Fastest?" by Robert Gray, January 1978.

Page 85: "If You Were a Bird," by Diane Watson, October 1974.

Library of Congress Cataloging in Publication Data

Main entry under title:

Ranger Rick's answer book.

Includes index.
Summary: Questions and answers about volcanoes, earthquakes, weather, animals, and plants.
1. Natural history—Miscellanea—Juvenile literature. [1. Natural history—Miscellanea. 2. Questions and answers] I. National Wildlife Federation.

QH48.R338   508   81-81734
ISBN 0-912186-40-2   AACR2

National Wildlife Federation

1400 16th Street, N.W.
Washington, D.C. 20036

Dr. Jay D. Hair
President

William W. Howard, Jr.
Executive Vice President

Staff for this Book

Howard F. Robinson
Editor

Victor H. Waldrop
Art Editor

Constance Brown Boltz
Art Director

Frank Fretz
Jean Pidgeon
Roz Schanzer
Illustrators

Rosa K. Hudson
Editorial Assistant

Priscilla Sharpless
Production Manager

Mariam Thayer Rutter
Production Artist

Margaret E. Wolf
Permissions Editor

Acknowledgments

The inquisitive members of
Ranger Rick's Nature Club who
have mailed questions to Wise Old
Owl were the inspiration behind
this book, and to them we are
greatly indebted. We also wish to
thank the staff of *Ranger Rick's
Nature Magazine,* especially Wise
Old Owl, for permission to reprint
many of their answers to the
club members' questions.